The American Influence on English Education

THE STUDENTS LIBRARY OF EDUCATION

The American Influence on English Education

by W. H. G. Armytage

Professor of Education
University of Sheffield

LONDON

ROUTLEDGE AND KEGAN PAUL

NEW YORK: HUMANITIES PRESS

To Claude Eggertsen

First published 1967
by Routledge and Kegan Paul Ltd
Broadway House, 68-74 Carter Lane
London, E.C.4

Printed in Great Britain
by Bookprint Limited
Crawley, Sussex

Library of Congress Catalog Card Number 67–18836

Contents

'Soap and education are not as sudden as a massacre, but they are more deadly in the long run' (Mark Twain, 1900, p. 350). Both, in their various ways, are intended to lower surface tension, ensure miscibility, and assist personal renovation. With education, if not with soap, the American ideal has been so much more attractive than the real; a phenomenon so common in other spheres of American life that G. K. Chesterton complained 'there is nothing the matter with the Americans except their ideals. The real American is all right; it is the ideal American who is all wrong' (*New York Times*, 1 February 1931). Wrong or not, that ideal has exercised a powerful influence over English educational policy over the last two centuries, even as it has itself changed. At times it has been used by reformers in much the same way as conservatives have used history. Today the very size of America enables it to rehearse problems we shall meet tomorrow.

Is there an optimal size and a maximal use of a school or college? A satisfactory method of training teachers? Are there adequately sophisticated batteries of attainment tests? or valid methods of vocational guidance? As these and other questions heave up on the rapidly expanding English educational front, eyes are turned to the United States. This, by now almost automatic, reflex action has marked English educational development over the last century and a half. What Englishmen saw, or thought they saw, and much more importantly, what they did as a result, is the subject of this book.

W.H.G.A.

The school as laboratory, the factory as laboratory, the prison as laboratory, these are essentially true conceptions, but their truth and their profit will be seen in America, in Germany—even in France—before they are grasped here.

(K. Pearson : *Life, Letters and Labour of
Francis Galton* (Cambrdge University Press, 1924))

I

The Yankee gospel

'I expect something from your New World, our Old World being as it were exhausted.' So a London Quaker merchant, Peter Collinson, apostrophised one of his American friends, and he had many. Among them was the very prototype of Yankees: Benjamin Franklin. Between them shuttled a regular exchange of books and apparatus; indeed Franklin's letters to Collinson on the subject of electricity became a classic, and his ideas on the subject so accepted that St. Paul's Cathedral was fitted in 1769 with lightning rods of his design.

Like his politics, Franklin's rods incurred the King's displeasure. So they were replaced by knobs, a change not welcome to the Royal Society, so the president resigned. That the Royal Society should support Franklin was not surprising, for he was a great promoter of organisations of scientists. His own particular creation, the American Philosophical Society, an intercolonial scientific organisation, anticipated the continental political union that fought for independence.

In England, too, he promoted societies which enrolled scientists for political purposes. His 'Club of Good Whigs' included scientists like Joseph Priestley, Dr. Price, and schoolmasters like James Burgh, John Canton and William

Rose, together with university teachers like Theophilus Lindsey (a pioneer of Sunday Schools long before Robert Raikes and John Jebb (a fervent opponent of religious tests in the universities). Focussed by the struggle with, and subsequent separation of, the American colonies, their ideas developed so quickly that James Burgh's *Political Disquisitions* (1774), has been described (Robbins, 1959, p. 365), as 'perhaps the most important political treatise which appeared in England in the first half of the reign of George III'. Burgh forecast the disaster which would follow unless parliament became more representative and the standing army was reduced.

Asked if he had read Burgh's book, another schoolmaster, Dr. Samuel Parr, is said to have replied: 'Have I read my Bible, Sir?' Poor Parr's own liberalism lost him the headmastership of Harrow and rendered his subsequent tenure of headmasterships of grammar schools at Colchester (1776–9) and Norwich (1779–85) most difficult. Parr was so great a friend of the chemist, Joseph Priestley, that later, in 1791, his house at Hatton in Warwickshire was thought to be threatened by the same mob that had destroyed Priestley's at Fairhill.

Another such society was formed in 1779 with Brand Hollis (a benefactor of Harvard) and William Jones (1746–1794), Jonathan Shipley's son-in-law, as leading members. This was the Society for Constitutional Information whose membership overlapped with that of a third, the Lunar Society of Birmingham. Thus, Thomas Day, author of *Sandford and Merton*, was a member of both. Day's enthusiasm for Rousseau was as great as for constitutional information and he urged members of the Society not to consult their 'private ease and safety'. And the Lunar Society had an American founder, Dr. Small, originally of William and Mary College in Virginia.

As Dr. Caroline Robbins concluded,

In the constitutions of the several United States many of the ideas of the Real Whigs found practical expression. A supreme court, rotation in office, a separation of powers, and a complete independence from each other of church and state fulfilled many a so-called utopian dream. The endless opportunities of the New World brought about a considerable degree of social equality if not an equality stabilised by an agrarian law.

(Robbins, 1959, pp. 210–1)

(ii)

Another Benjamin, reared not many miles away from Franklin in the same utilitarian spirit, was Benjamin Thompson. Like Franklin, he was interested in the manufacture of fireplaces. Also like Franklin, he was elected F.R.S. But whereas Benjamin Franklin remained an American, Benjamin Thompson left America for Europe after the War of Independence, where his domestic inventions—fire-grates, lamps, soups and coffee-pots—ensured respectful attention. And whereas Franklin's scientific associates gravitated towards his Whiggish principles, Thompson set about ridding the Bavarian Academy of Sciences of republican ones. With a crisp and ominous efficiency, he also reorganised the Bavarian army and employed it to build a workhouse for beggars and a botanical garden, in which cottages and farmhouses were built as models, stocked with specially selected cattle 'con cealed in a thick wood behind a public coffee house'. His work for the poor in Munich had attracted attention in England where yet another American, Sir Thomas Bernard, had formed with others a Society for Bettering the Condition of the Poor. Thompson told him:

Go on, my dear Sir, and be assured that when you have put doing good in fashion you will have done all that human wisdom can do to retard and prolong the decline of a great and powerful nation that has arrived at or passed the zenith of human glory.

3

He told Bernard to make the poor useful by educating them:

> there must be something to *see* and *touch* otherwise people in general will have but faint, imperfect and transitory ideas of those important and highly interesting objects with which you must make them acquainted in order to become zealous converts to our new philosophy and useful members of our community.

Appointed as Bavarian Ambassador to Britain, Thompson proved unacceptable to King George III, so he came to London as a private citizen. At a committee meeting of the Society for Bettering the Condition of the Poor, he dilated upon the importance of diffusing ideas concerning domestic comfort and convenience, and the application of science to arts and manufactures. The best medium, he suggested, was a teaching laboratory, with a museum and exhibition, sustained by subscriptions, fees and donations.

English manufacturers objected to making the very latest ideas so freely available to all and sundry. As their spokesman, young Matthew Boulton, son of the great Birmingham steam-engine pioneer, said, 'however much support he (Thompson) received from the male and female nobility his scheme would not be relished by the British manufacturer.' Others objected to the working class being admitted to a 'school for mechanics'. One of Rumford's appointees was told that his plan 'to instruct the lower classes in science must be dropped as quietly as possible' and that if he persisted he would 'become a marked man'.

Such criticism notwithstanding, the scheme took shape in 1800 as the Royal Institution. As a church for spreading the Yankee gospel in England, it was a great success, sustaining, amongst others, Sir Humphrey Davy and Michael Faraday. It sprang from Thompson's work in Munich, where he had been led to consider the idea of 'an

Institution for introducing and bringing forward into general use, new inventions and improvements, particularly such as relate to the Management of Heat and the Saving of Fuel'.

(iii)

In addition to Benjamin Thompson, two other returning loyalists who contributed to English education during this period were Francis Green and Lindley Murray.

Like Thompson, Francis Green came from Massachusetts. He established, near London, a charitable school for teaching the deaf, described as 'the first of its kind in the English speaking world'. (Curti, 1963, p. 8.) He went on to translate the writings of the Abbé de l'Epée, the great French experimenter in this field, in 1803. The needs of his own deaf-mute son led him to return to America, where his efforts in this field intensified till his death six years later.

Lindley Murray, on the other hand, came from Pennsylvania and settled at Holgate, near York, where he built a botanical garden, said to exceed Kew in variety, and compiled an *English Grammar* on what might almost be called botanical principles. This grammar was a huge success, for from first publication in 1795 it ran to nearly fifty editions and was widely used in both England and America (Lyman, 1922). An abridgement, issued in 1797, went to 120 editions, each of ten thousand. Spelling Books on French grammar followed. His friend, the chemist John Dalton, considered them 'the worst of all the contrivances invented by human ingenuity for puzzling the brains of the young'.

(iv)

Meanwhile, the American frontier needed servicing by professionally trained people for whom colleges were provided by the various churches or on the initiative of individual states. So Washington (1782), Hampden-Sidney (1776), Transylvania (1780), Dickinson (1773), St. John's (1784), Franklin and Marshall (1787), Williams (1785), Bowdoin (1794) and Union (1785) and Middlebury (1800), were supplemented by the earliest state universities like Georgia (1785), North Carolina (1789), Vermont (1791) and Tennessee (1794). Poor and meagre these foundations might be, but as each new state was admitted into the Union, Congress was encouraged to make land grants for more. Two such land grant colleges at Athens (1804) and Miami University at Oxford (1809) were established by Ohio. Others arose as the new republic doubled in size with the Louisiana Purchase (1803) and the purchase of Florida. Thanks to the rapid application of steam to navigation (pioneered by John Fitch and Robert Fulton), and textiles (thanks to Slater's spinning mill of 1791 and Whitney's cotton gin of 1793), these colleges grew till by just before the Civil War 182 permanent colleges and universities had been founded, to say nothing of many more which were to go out of existence (Tewkesbury, 1932).

Britons took stock of this when thirty-four-year-old Francis Gilmer came to London in October 1824, to recruit talent for Jefferson's sectarian university of Virginia. His hosts included Lord Brougham, Leonard Horner, George Birkbeck, Major Cartwright and Thomas Campbell: the very group who were, three years later, to establish England's first non-sectarian university. There is no doubt that they were influenced by Jefferson's blueprint of a university free to students of all denominations. Up to Gilmer's arrival, most reformers had been content either to campaign, in a rather half-hearted way, against the religious tests which made Oxford and Cambridge preserves of the national church or to compromise with injustice by sending their sons to Scottish or European universities.

Gilmer's English hosts were tuned in to American

developments. Thomas Campbell's father was in the Virginia trade, his elder brother was living in Richmond and another brother had married the daughter of Patrick Henry. To him, as to his colleagues, Gilmer appeared as 'a fellow in the new faith, and what was more, a witness to the practicability of what men said was a dream. That which was done at Charlottesville could surely be done in London.' (Hale Bellott, 1929, p. 16.)

So it was. No religious test barred students from entering the new University of London in 1827. And those working for universities in other parts of England, like James Yates, took heart. Yates, later to be the first secretary to the Council of the British Association for the Advancement of Science, pleaded very powerfully for universities in the North and West of England which should be untrammelled by sectarian tests. He symbolised the orientation towards America of the intellectual antennae of the great industrial north of England.

Even Charles Dickens (whose *Martin Chuzzlewit* was certainly no advertisement for the Americans) was moved to applaud the non-denominational character of American colleges and universities:

> They disseminate no prejudices; rear no bigots; dig up the buried ashes of no old superstitions; never interpose between people and their improvement; exclude no man because of his religious opinions; and above all, in their whole course of study and instruction, recognise a world . . . beyond the college walls.
>
> (*American Notes*, 1867, p. 10)

(v)

If Jefferson could be described as 'in fact and perhaps unknowingly the leader of a secret resistance movement in Europe during the Empire and Bourbon restoration' (Spiller, Thorpe, Johnson and Canby, 1948, p. 209),

Franklin could be regarded as the posthumous patron saint of the industrious artisan. Early in 1824, a Franklin institute was established at Philadelphia by S. V. Merrick, assisted by Dr. W. H. Keating who had just come from England. Other institutes followed in Baltimore (1825), and Boston (1827). In smaller towns a more characteristic American mutant appeared: the lyceum, where entertainment sugared the educational pill and the presence of women enabled classes in spinning, sewing and housecraft to be organised. These lyceums were cited by Sir Thomas Wyse, the irrepressible Irish advocate of educational reform in England, as having something to contribute to the Mechanics' Institutes in England. He may not have been believed when he said that 'thousands of [American] children of not more than eight or ten years old, know more geology, mineralogy, botany, statistical facts etc., of what concerns their daily and national interests and occupations, than was probably known thirty years ago by any five individuals in the United States', but his enthusiastic endorsement of the lyceums was probably responsible for their catching on in Lancashire. For in 1839, the year in which he wrote these words, lyceums were organised in Ancoats, Chorlton-on-Medwick and Salford followed by a fourth in Oldham a year later.

Certainly 'an account of the salutary effect produced by the establishment of mechanics' libraries in several States of the Union' written by Sheriff Noah of New York to Egerton Smith of Liverpool led to 'a mechanics' and apprentices' library' being founded in Liverpool. Further examples of American stimulus to such movements abound. Dr. James Black of Kentucky came to London in 1834 and met William Lovett, then interested in improving working men's education. According to one account he 'induced' Lovett to form the London Working Men's Association. (Dobbs, 1919, p. 227.) Pervading all these was the spirit of Benjamin Franklin, as the 'hymn' of the Franklin Club formed at Barnsley in 1843 indicates:

Degraded churls, why listless stand?
The work of progress needs a hand.
The Franklin Club will lead the van
In striving for the rights of man.

Five years after its foundation it had 220 members as compared to 184 in the Mechanics' Institute and 137 in the Church Institute (Popple, 1959, p. 32).

(vi)

One of the most popular authors in these Mechanics' Institutes was Ralph Waldo Emerson, the Boston Unitarian. Amongst those who flocked to welcome him when he visited England in 1848 were the secretaries of the Mechanics' Institutes at Liverpool (W. B. Hodgson) and Huddersfield (G. S. Phillips), the president of the Nottingham People's College (Joseph Neuberg), a lecturer in the Government School of Design at Newcastle upon Tyne (W. B. Scott), and the great Tynemouth bridgemaker George Crawshay, who supported the Poles, Hungarians, Danes and Chartists with the same intensity as he did the ninety bridges he made for the Caucasian railway.

James Hutchison Stirling spoke for many when he told Emerson:

Your works form large part of my circulating current . . . Carlyle came first, but, by and by, I used to prattle of him to myself as but the eagle (of imaginative intellect say) that flew away with me to the rock Emerson —rock (shall we say again?) of moral thought. . . . Lastly, I have had intercourse with many 'for whom history has no tablets'—simple students—humble men —with whom, nevertheless, your works had penetrated with due effect—raising them into quietude and sincerity and thought.

(Scudder, 1936, p. 211)

9

The 'Emerson mania', as *The English Review* called it in 1849, propelled liberal thinkers along another line after the alarms and excursions of Chartism. At Coventry, Charles Bray hailed 'the advent of the original veridical man himself' and recorded that he had 'met no man to whom I got so much attached in so short a time'. (Bray, 1883, p. 72.) Bray, a Coventry ribbon manufacturer and owner of the *Coventry Herald*, was deeply interested in experiments in co-operative living then taking place on the American continent, as his *Outline of Social Systems and Communities* (1844) indicates. He also strongly supported ameliorative groups nearer home, like the Coventry Labour and Artisans' Society. At his house, twenty-nine-year-old Mary Ann Evans (later known as George Eliot) met Emerson and noted in her diary 'the first *man* I have ever seen'. For to Emerson, factory and railway fell 'within the great Order not less than the beehive or the spider's geometrical web. Nature adopts them very fast into her vital circles, and the gliding train of cars she loves like her own.' He found enthusiastic disciples in the industrial north of England, whom his friend Carlyle so dismissively described as 'a poor washy set of people chiefly "friends of humanity" to keep wide away from whom is my most necessary struggle'. But Carlyle did not like Americans either. 'They have begotten', he told Cobden, 'with a rapidity beyond recorded example, eighteen millions of the greatest *bores* ever seen in this world before—that hitherto is their feat in History' (Scudder, 1936, p. 171).

These English disciples of Emerson's were strengthened in their faith by his pastoral visit in 1848. Collectively, they challenged the materialist inertia and spiritual sluggishness he detected and recorded in his *English Traits* (1856). The first of them, Alexander Ireland, who had organised Emerson's visit, published and managed the *Manchester Examiner*, a liberal organ which from its first issue in 1846 to the last in 1890 never ceased supporting liberal causes. Ireland himself was one of the seven founders of the Lancashire Public School Association in 1847, and three years later saw it transformed into the National Public Schools Association. He also helped purchase the Hall of Science at Campfield in 1850 and open it as the Manchester Free Library in 1852.

Almost as effective was another disciple, George Dawson, a schoolmaster's son and a teacher himself, whose Emersonian sermons led his Birmingham congregation to build a chapel for him known as the Church of the Saviour so that he could preach the example of Christ. 'Special organisations on novel lines were used for the education of children and the care of the poor', wrote his biographer, 'with night classes for adults' (Ireland, 1882). Having accompanied Emerson through the barricades in Paris in 1848, he, like Ireland, followed his master's precepts in supporting the establishment of public libraries and secular schools, giving evidence to the public libraries committee in 1849, and later taking an active part in the deliberations of the Birmingham School Board.

A third was Samuel Lucas, brother-in-law of John Bright, owner of a cotton mill and author of a *Plan for the Establishment of a General System of Secular Education in the County of Lancashire* (1847). He was later to edit the *Morning Star*, and his wife, after a visit to America, was to become a crusader for women's suffrage.

To the efforts of these Emersonians for the establishment of school boards were added those of others whom we must now consider.

2

The emergence of the school boards

Admiration for American schools was long felt. After twelve years in New York, a Wykehamist lawyer, John Bristed, confessed: 'They surpass all other nations in *elementary* education; that is to say, in imparting the rudiments of instruction to the people at large.' He considered that

> Both countries would be highly benefited by borrowing from each other; England by adopting the American system of instructing *all* the people, and the United States by cultivating that higher species of learning, which has rendered the English scholars, for a series of ages, so particularly pre-eminent.
>
> (Bristed, 1815, pp. 318–9, 327–9)

Bristed took a very sane view of the United States of the early nineteenth century. To him it was 'neither the garden of Eden nor the valley of Tophet'. He deplored the picture projected by Gilbert Imlay and M. St. John de Crevecœur wherein the United States appeared as 'the abode of *more* than all the perfection of innocence, happiness, plenty, learning and wisdom, than *can* be allotted to human beings to enjoy'. Such pictures, however, were increasingly projected as political debate ebbed and flowed in Britain, when to write a book about, for or against, America was to declare one's political allegiance. Democracy was a smear word to English writers like Captain Marryat (1839) and Captain Basil Hall (1829), but to James Stuart it was such an exemplar that his picture in *Three Years in North America* (1832) was described by the Vice-Chancellor of the newly-founded London University as 'partiality amounting to prejudice'. On these grounds it was banned by the Lincoln Mechanics' Institute (Armytage, 1949).

Stuart's book, on the other hand, was considered by Richard Cobden to be 'the most matter-of-fact and impartial' of all those written on America. Cobden confirmed its findings by visiting the United States himself, and noting in his diary when he visited an infant school in New York:

Oh happy sight, pregnant with hopes of the exaltation of the character of future generations! I hereby dedicate myself to the task of promoting the cause of infant schools in England where they may become an instrument for ameliorating the fate of the children working in the factories whose case I fear is beyond the reach of all other remedies.

(Cawley, 1952, p. 121)

He told a friend:

every American of whatever shade of politics will avow that his hopes of the permanency of sound democratic self-government, free from anarchy on the one hand and tyranny on the other, are based entirely upon the great and increasing knowledge of the masses:—*education—education—education* is the motto of every enlightened democrat in America.

(Cawley, 1952, p. 26)

So education became, for Cobden, 'the only public matter' upon which he felt 'disposed to put on' his 'armour for another seven years war'. His first seven years war ended in 1846 with the repeal of the Corn Laws. The second opened with the formation of the Lancashire Public Schools Association.

This pressure group, itself a legatee of the Anti-Corn Law League, had the avowed intention of securing the adoption of the Massachusetts system in England. Cobden told his phrenological friend George Combe in 1850: 'I shall now go straight at the mark and shall neither give nor take quarter. I have made up my mind to go for the Massachusetts system as nearly as we can get it' (Cawley, 1952, p. 27). Four years later, he was asking his old political ally, John Bright, to take sides: 'You can't take a neutral part or a lukewarm attitude. Is not the time come to declare for the New England system?'

Anyone who reinforced the case earned his thanks. When the railway magnate, Sir Edward Watkin, came out on his side he told him that he

> could not have done a wiser and more patriotic service than to make the people of this country better acquainted with what is going on in the United States. . . . To shut our eyes to what is going on there is almost as sage a proceeding as that of an ostrich when he puts his head under a sand-heap.
>
> (Cawley, 1952, p. 34)

(ii)

The American system was based on popularly elected school boards administering non-sectarian schools for everyone. It owed much to the mothers of Ohio, the first state in the Union to receive the congressional land grant for schools in each of its townships. Admitted in 1803, eighteen years after the Survey Ordinance, Ohio schools got under way after 1837, when Samuel Lewis, as superintendent of common schools, supplemented the land grant by allowing districts to levy taxes. As a lawyer Lewis believed that to open a school was to close a jail. At the same time, Massachusetts appointed Horace Mann, and Connecticut Henry Barnard to do likewise. Mann conducted an imaginative campaign in the columns of the *Common School Journal* and enlisted scientists like Agassiz in his support.

The connection between Massachusetts and the English reformers was a close one, for Horace Mann was a disciple of George Combe. Indeed, just as he was about to take over the public schools of Massachusetts he read Combe's *Constitution of Man*, which he considered would 'work a revolution in mental science equal to that which Lord Bacon had worked in natural science'. (Hinsdale, 1898, p. 95.)

For Combe showed, to Mann's satisfaction, that character and motives were connected with physical predispositions (which could be predicted from 'bumps' on the head), and that these could be modified by education. Combe tried to free teaching from empiricism, and encourage the use of physiology and psychology. He held that education should be practical, and that the teachers could be developed through appropriate exercise and activity. His impact on Mann was such that Mann's biographer remarks:

it is difficult for one who looks over the whole ground to resist the conviction that the measure of truth found in the *pseudo*-science did much more to fit him for his great educational work than his earlier readings of Brown and other metaphysicians.

(Hinsdale, 1898, p. 102)

As Mann himself saw, 'the absence of tradition and convention and the freedom of Western Society—the fact that the ground was unencumbered, enabled local superintendents and the public schools to bulk more significantly in public esteem' (Hinsdale, 1898, p. 294).

(iii)

Impressed by what he, too, had seen in America, Combe nailed his colours to the mast of the *Edinburgh Review* with a warmly favourable description of 'Education in the State of Massachusetts' in 1841. Others joined in. The public relations organiser of the early Victorian liberals, James Silk Buckingham, considered that teachers in New York were better than those employed by the voluntary societies in England, then providing the only elementary education for the masses in England (Buckingham, 1841, i. pp. 203–4). A North Country chemist and co-founder of the British Association for the Advancement of Science pointed out fourteen years later that the educational budget of New York State alone was larger than that of England, whilst that of Connecticut and Rhode Island was even larger (Johnstone, 1851, ii. p. 491).

Philadelphia, too, excited admiration. Alexander MacKay, a Scotsman who was employed by the *London Morning Chronicle*, described its 1,660 school districts and 80,000 pupils with admiration in 1850. The young Lord Acton, who held no high opinion of American institutions, kept his thoughts to himself, and did not publish his diary, but even he remarked that teaching positions in Philadelphia were paid so well that it was not uncommon for a minister to renounce his orders for teaching (Acton, 1922, cxi. p. 80).

One of the most widely read English authors, Harriet Martineau, who stayed in the United States for two years (1836–38), found the provision of schools to be so adequate that the only children seen about were truants (Martineau, 1837, ii. p. 269). J. R. Godley, a Tory, confessed himself 'astonished' at the literary proficiency of the negro pupils and their negro teachers in New York, and remarked that their speaking and writing was far superior to that of the English working classes (Godley, 1844, ii. pp. 33–4).

Observers even more prejudiced than Godley agreed that American schools enabled those who rose in the social scale not to feel inferior to those they met on the way up. Mrs. Bishop in 1854, H. A. Murray in 1855 and T. C. Grattan in 1859, the first a young lady, the second a naval captain and the third a former British consul, all regarded the common school as one of the 'glories of America'.

(iv)

As a model, American board schools were held up for admiration in numerous debates in the House of Commons. The fiery diminutive radical J. A. Roebuck set the precedent for this, as for so much else, when he introduced the first bill for a comprehensive system of national education in 1833. From then, until 1870, when a lesser variant finally passed into law, numerous bills were mangled in the House acccompanied by invocations of, and imprecations against, American precedents.

Three examples must suffice. In stressing how education could strengthen the arms of the police and regulate the poor, Roebuck cited on 30 July 1833 Livingstone's prison code in Louisiana. Pitching his argument higher, he continued:

In America, the magnificent provisions for this same great object surpass all that the world has seen before. The single state of New York has dedicated to the advancement of knowledge a prospective revenue that must shortly surpass the whole revenue of the state and more than equal to the enormous sums which we lavish upon our Government. (*Hansard*, 30 July 1833)

Introducing a similarly comprehensive measure for

Ireland on 19 March 1835, Sir Thomas Wyse urged members to 'Look to Germany, look to France—look even to America.' Finally, when the 'Massachusetts plan' of the N.P.S.A. was introduced in a bill by William Johnson Fox on 17 April 1850, his supporter, David Hume, urged his hearers to 'Look to the United States and say if secular education has produced the evils foreshadowed by the noble Lord at the head of the government.' Roebuck followed up by asking whether the House 'would repudiate this experience on the ground that this people were not Englishmen? Why, if ever there was a body of people who deserved the name it was the people of new England . . . the most moral and religious people on the face of the globe' (*Hansard*, 17 April 1850).

So strong were American precedents that the voluntary societies, then monopolising elementary education in England, invoked Horace Mann's reports as arguments against such secular education being adopted in England, citing the views of a government inspector, Hugh Seymour Tremenheere, that American precedents in secular control 'cannot be referred to as a solution of our own difficulties or as a safe guide upon a path upon which we have not yet entered' (*Hansard*, 10 April 1856). In rebuttal, Richard Monckton Milnes (later Lord Houghton) replied:

> Those who said in an invidious sense that the American system of education was purely secular, committed a grave error, because in truth the people of the United States had separated the religious element from the secular mainly in order that the former might receive more careful attention; and certainly no nation in the world was possessed of more profound religious convictions or was more activated by religious principles than our Transatlantic kinsmen. (*Hansard*, 10 April 1856)

Wisely, Sir James Pakington did not confine himself to praising only the American system. His argument was that instead of England having only one country better than itself, there were not above three or four countries in Europe in a worse position. Pakington got his way, when in 1859 a Royal Commission was appointed to examine elementary education: the Newcastle Commission. Its report led to the Revised Code, basing grants to the denominational schools on their results, externally assessed. Its architect, Robert Lowe, considered the chief advantage of the system of payment by results to be that 'it tended very forcibly to the secularisation of education' (Tropp, 1957, p. 180).

(v)

After the Revised Code got under way, another Royal Commission, appointed to examine the various endowed schools in England, called for a full-scale report on American common schools.

The author of the report was the Rev. James Fraser (later Bishop of Manchester), who spent five months in 1865—from 2 May to 4 October—in New York, just as the Civil War drew to a close. Indeed, Fraser considered that 'if there had been a free-school system in the South there would have been no secession, no civil war'. 'We do not turn to America to copy their institutions in a servile manner', he wrote, quoting De Tocqueville, 'but rather to learn.' And he learned that 'every American citizen has to play a part in the great arena of public life, which in other countries is reserved for the governing class or classes'. Whereas:

A practical education for a Hindoo Sudra, an English factory operative or miner, a Russian serf, or a Mexican peon is not that which an American citizen should receive. *They* have nothing to do with the affairs of Government. The State neither needs their counsel nor asks their advice. It requires them to be industrious, quiet, content. The warp and woof of our entire system of government is spun and woven by the citizens. (Fraser, 1856, p. 159)

Fraser was quite frank in his assessment of the relative merits of English and American schools:

An American pupil probably leaves school with more special knowledge but with less general development. He would have more acquaintance (not very profound, though), with certain branches of physical science, perhaps more, certainly as much, acquaintance with mathematics, but not more acquaintance with modern languages, and much less acquaintance with the ancient languages and classical literature. I think our best teachers are better (perhaps because more regularly educated) than their best, but our worst teachers are incomparably worse, duller, more un-methodical, more indolent, more uninteresting than anything I saw or can conceive of being tolerated among them. (Fraser, 1866, p. 172)

He continued:

An American teacher may be immoral, ignorant, and in many ways incompetent, but he, and particularly she, could hardly be dull. Liveliness and energy, hiding sometimes behind a multitude of other sins, seem to be their inherent qualities. I saw in America many in-efficient schools, but the drowsy dullness of the teacher and the inattentive habits of the children, which characterise so many an English school, I never saw. Fraser, 1866, p. 173)

He concluded of the Americans:

It is no flattery to say that it is, if not the most *highly* educated, yet certainly the most *generally* educated and intelligent people on the earth. (Fraser, 1886, p. 203)

20

(vi)

On the basis of Fraser's report, Jesse Collings, a Birmingham reformer, wrote *An Outline of the American Schools System: with Remarks on the Establishment of Common Schools in England* (1868). He also proposed the formation of a society, on the lines of the N.P.S.A., to agitate for free and secular schools on the American model. So with the help of Joseph Chamberlain (a friend of Emerson's brother) and George Dixon the National Education League was formed. Strongly supported by British manufacturers, this great pressure group employed an army of speakers and writers who, in the words of its secretary

> more often referred to the schools in Boston than those of any other city. The reason for this has been that in this city only have been found in practice three of the most essential features of the scheme advocated by the League—representative government, free admission and compulsory school attendance. (Adams, 1882, p. 256)

The League rapidly established branches all over the country. Thus, the chairman of the Ipswich branch was a radical Anglican clergyman, the Rev. F. Barham Zincke, a veteran campaigner for universal education whose convictions had been strengthened by a visit to America in 1868. In the London branch, a leading spirit who accompanied the League's deputation to the Government was Sir Charles Dilke, grandson of a 'Godwin perfectibility man' who held that America would 'be the country to take up the human intellect where England leaves off' (Forman, 1952, p. 234) and son of a promoter of the industrial exhibitions of 1851 and 1853. Like Zincke, Dilke had also recently returned from America and his account of his visit, *Greater Britain* (1868), was described by John Stuart Mill as the product of a mind 'predisposed to the most advanced and enlightened views on the principal questions of the future' (Jenkins, 1958, p. 43).

When W. E. Forster (who had served his political apprenticeship on the N.P.S.A.), became Vice-President of the Council in 1868, he drafted an education bill to satisfy the need for a national system of schools. Alerted by *The Times* (then printed on Boston-made presses), debaters on the merits of his bill in 1870 were alive to the fundamental principle that school boards on the American model were to be established to fill up the gaps in the existing provision offered by voluntary schools. As the leading spokesman of the League, Sir Charles Dilke helped to prevent the School Boards being committees of the vestries (as was originally proposed), and to secure that they were elected by balloting the rate-payers.

Since, apart from the establishment of school boards, the rest of the League's programme—free schools and compulsion especially—was inadequately met by the Act, the secretary, Francis Adams, felt it incumbent upon him 'to supply for English reformers the means of insight into the operation of the American System of Elementary Education'. He warned his readers that 'international comparisons are now forced upon all countries by international competition'.

Either then, the American system has produced a satisfactory result, or else a conspiracy on a grand scale has been entered into by travellers from all nations, including such observers as De Tocqueville and Fraser, to deceive the world as to the measure of intelligence and information in the United States. (Adams, 1875, p. 229)

Adams now found himself defending further development of the board schools on two fronts: the voluntaryists and those opposed to free education. For voluntaryists spoke up the bluff Johnsonian Methodist Dr. J. H. Rigg, who had opposed the handing over of Wesleyan schools to the boards. Spokesman of the other group was the blind Professor Fawcett, who argued that if the demand for free education were not resisted 'encouragement would be given to socialism in its most baneful form'. Rigg confessed that he 'differed more from the Birmingham school than any other' and insisted that 'in nearly one half of the United States no efficient system of public schools is in operation' (Rigg, 1823, p. 93).

vii

Looking back at these days from the hindsight of 1902, Goldwin Smith observed to Lord Mount Stephen:

It is all very well to eulogise the American school system, but what would the United States do if they did not draw rough labour from abroad? How many Americans would work in the mines, or on railroads, or go into domestic service? (Haultain, 1913, p. 385)

A considerable proportion of this labour from abroad came from Britain. From 1843–1853 70 per cent (150,000) of British emigrants went to America. Subsequent decades showed little diminution: 61 per cent (100,000), 72 per cent (113,000), 64.9 per cent (109,000), 67.2 per cent (172,000) and 65.5 per cent (114,000). From 1901 to 1911 it was 44.4 per cent (126,000) and from 1911 to 1913 26.5 per cent (123,000) (Thomas, 1954, p. 57).

To the author of *Tom Brown's Schooldays* this hegira of the artisans seemed likely to increase, unless the franchise was extended. 'We shall,' he forecast, 'at last lose the pith and marrow of the working class who contribute so largely to the wealth and prosperity of the country' (*Hansard*, 19 April 1866).

3
Mass literacy

(i)

The immediate and visible consequence of the common
school was publicised as, and believed to be, universal
literacy. By ministering to this in Philadelphia, William
Cobbett found a mission in life, and returned to Britain
in 1800 to found that most effective organ of popular
radicalism, *The Weekly Political Register*. In 1816, fourteen years after its first issue, he reduced its price to 2d,
saying:

> Many a father will thus, I hope, be induced to spend
> his evenings at home in instructing his children in the
> history of their misery, and in warming them into acts
> of patriotism. (Aspinall, 1949, p. 45)

Instead of attending divine service, reported one of the
government spies, 'the Sundays of the people [in Lanca-
shire] were occupied in reading the works of Cobbett and
Paine and other similar publications' (Simon, 1960,
p. 187). The heavy Stamp Tax on newspapers led to the
foundation of newsrooms. Some editors, anxious to increase their circulation, clamoured for a free press and
a literate public.

Here the literate American with his free press appeared

as 'a trumpet to the mouth of freedom'. Bulwer Lytton, the prolific, energetic and observant Conservative novelist, argued that if English newspapers could circulate as freely and widely as their American counterparts, the people would not be as helpless as they were. Indeed, he told the House of Commons:

> there is not a town in America with 10,000 inhabitants that has not its daily paper. Boston, which has only half the population of Liverpool, puts forth 10 times as many publications. Pennsylvania publishes 1 newspaper to every 4 inhabitants, the British Isles 1 to every 36. (*Hansard*, 14 June 1832)

Even the reduction of the penal Stamp Tax to a penny in 1836 seemed only to kindle desire for its total abolition, and a completely free press on the transatlantic model, since 'An American press', as Cobden told Bright on 7 September 1852, 'would do more to educate the millions than all the schoolmasters in the land' (Cawley, 1952, p. 29).

So the advice he gave to the group working for total repeal of the Stamp Tax was to make it an education question: 'put the *education-loving* Government in a crucible from which they never can escape, with the dross of the Taxes on Knowledge sticking to them' (Collett, 1899, i. 205).

The British press became even more Americanised when the Stamp Tax was finally abolished during the Crimean War, since the increased demand meant greater mechanisation, so that by 1867, almost all the leading newspapers in Great Britain and Northern Ireland were being printed on American Hoe machines (Dunning, 1958, p. 18).

Devised to cope with American mass circulation, Hoe presses provided, after the 1870 Act opened the eyes of literacy to Englishmen, a golden opportunity for Alfred Harmsworth. Drawing freely on American newspapers and magazines for articles and paragraphs, he issued his first paper, *Answers*, in 1888. Later he exploited American style, layout and methods of presentation for his *Daily Mail* (1896) and *Daily Mirror* (1903). He later got control of *The Times*, where he found that Americanisms were creeping in ahead of him. So he warned his employees in 1909:

> Above all do not use any Americanism . . . Somebody should stand by with a coke-hammer and smash every American and other foreign word that tries to get into the building. Our own language is quite good enough. American is very amusing to talk, but it should not be allowed to be printed in *The Times*. (Pound and Harmsworth, 1959, p. 347)

But it was trying to stop a flood. A generation earlier, the purist John Ruskin told readers of his newsletter:

> when in this letter I have used an American expression, or ought like one, there came upon you a sense of sudden wrong—the darting through you of acute cold, I meant you to feel like that; for it is the essential function of America to make us feel like that.

Ruskin wrote to another newspaper in 1877:

> Don't attempt to learn from America. An Englishman has brains enough to discover for himself what is good for England; and should learn, when he is to be taught anything, from his fathers, not from his children.

Though in a much better position than Ruskin to stop such Americanisation (to emphasise the process, the last word should be spelt with a z), Harmsworth could not. In spite of his objections to terms like 'check up', 'try out', 'win out', 'typewriter operator' and 'elevator', he found that even *The Times* was 'getting quite American.

26

Yesterday in a headline, we had the term "speeded up" '
(Pound and Harmsworth, 1959, p. 617).

His and other English newspapers adopted the comic
strip. However much national pride might be salved by
quoting Egyptian papyri, Greek ceramics, the Bayeux
tapestry, Hogarth or Cruikshank, the fact remains that
the comic strip was born in the New York newspaper
world of the 1890's. Indeed, the first bona-fide comic strip
was 'The Yellow Kid' in the *New York World*, who wore
a bright yellow dress on which words appeared. This gave
the phrase 'yellow press' to the journals relying on
comics: a phrase now recognised by the Oxford English
Dictionary (Mott, 1962, p. 525).

(ii)

The instruments of American literacy were its juvenile
books, mass-produced for American homes. To offset the
'horror' element in nursery tales like Blue Beard, Mother
Goose, Jack the Giant Killer and Red Riding Hood (which
seemed to be 'written for children with the express purpose of reconciling them to vice and crime'), Samuel
Goodrich wrote his famous Peter Parley series, working
at them, it is said, for fourteen hours a day and earning
the supreme compliment of being plagiarised. The first of
a hundred similar volumes was *The Tales of Peter Parley
about America* (1827). 'Probably no "juvenile" author',
wrote F. J. Harvey Darton (1958, p. 233), 'purporting or
appearing to be one person, has ever had so large a
circulation of so many books in so short a period.'

The even more famous McGuffey Readers, named after
a young professor who laboured to secure the passage of
the law under which the common schools of Ohio were
organised, had a fantastic circulation of well over a
hundred and twenty million copies. If Ohio was the
cradle of the common school, it was also the cradle of
the really mass-produced textbook.

27

The distinctive 'American' atmosphere of some of these books, especially of the 'Rollo' Series—some 180 volumes by Jacob Abbott—so worried some Anglican clergymen, that J. H. Newman composed a special *Tract for the Times*—Number 73 (1836) *Ad Scholas*—castigating them. One of England's fêted progressive teachers, Charles Mayo, founder of a Pestalozzian school at Cheam, found Abbott's outlook too permissive, and considered Abbott's pupils to be 'too much persuaded or coaxed to adopt the master's views'. Mayo considered that Abbott 'exercised too little authority' and his pupils learned 'too little submission' (Abbott, 1834, p. 18).

Such criticism notwithstanding, Abbott's English admirers included the Headmaster of Rugby, who expressed 'much delight' after reading some of Abbott's stories, and described them as 'enjoying a large circulation in England'. This, coming from one who 'abhorred' the spirit of the American war of independence and felt 'unable to sympathise' with 'the historical liberty' that grew out of the middle ages, was a great tribute. 'Nothing can save us from falling in to the American system', lamented Arnold, 'they will take our place in the world, I think not unworthily, though with far less advantage in many respects than those which we have so fatally wasted' (Stanley, 1890, pp. 207, 210, 227).

But the real point was that Abbott and other American authors wrote for children who were not being given a lower class education. This was clearly seen by Charles Mayo:

If we think that working classes in America are too much disposed to a rude assertion of equality with their richer neighbours, must we not admit that the wealthy and high-born of England are too much inclined to regard the lower orders as an inferior race of beings? . . . It is however beginning to be seen, not only that we ought not, but that we dare not neglect the lower classes of society. Their growing influence we cannot overthrow; it remains for us to turn it into the right channels . . . It is clear, however, that no such fruits can be expected from the National School System. Its utter inadequacy to meet the normal wants of the people, and to train up a decent and well-informed community, is mournfully evident (Abbott, 1834, pp. v–vi).

(iii)

The menace presented by Jacob Abbott to the young was paralleled by that of Emerson to their elders, and it is no coincidence that in the very year in which Newman attacked Abbott, Emerson should have published *Nature*. It was not the eloquent sensitivity with which the Boston Unitarian praised the new technology so much as his vision that man would transcend technology by rationally defining its ends, that disturbed more orthodox Englishmen.

The land [said Emerson] is the appointed remedy for what is false and fantastic in our culture . . . its tranquillizing sanative influence, is to repair the errors of a scholastic and traditional education, and bringing us into just relations with men and things. (Marx, 1964, pp. 229–241)

Emerson represented a direct threat to Anglicanism, as its diminutive but irrepressible publicist, Charles Kingsley, saw and said in three books. Kingsley's own brother-in-law, J. A. Froude, after writing a life of St. Neot for Newman's *Lives of the English Saints* in 1844, lapsed from the Church of England after reading Emerson and resigned his Oxford Fellowship. 'He broke the fetters,' confessed Froude, 'I owe my freedom to him' (Gohdes, 1944, p. 145).

In the same way, only later, Edward Carpenter abandoned orders as a result of reading Emerson's disciple,

29

Walt Whitman. 'Life', wrote Carpenter, 'deep down was flowing out and away from the surroundings and traditions amid which I lived—a current of sympathy carrying it westward, across the Atlantic.' Visits to Whitman in 1877 and 1884 confirmed Carpenter in his belief in Whitman as a prophet-seer. The discipleship was so obvious that Carpenter's own book, *Toward Democracy*, was described by Havelock Ellis as 'Whitman and water' (Gohdes, 1944, pp. 143-8).

If Canon Kingsley disliked Emerson, he detested Whitman as 'a coarse sensual mind' (Blodgett, 1934, p. 204). Even Matthew Arnold was moved to comment that 'few stocks could be trusted to grow up properly without having a priesthood and an aristocracy to act as their schoolmaster'. Arnold was horrified at Whitman's conviction that democratic America would renew civilisation and insisted that 'we may greatly require to keep, as if it were our life, the doctrine that we are failures after all, if we cannot eschew vain boasting and vain imaginations' (Allott, 1953, p. 64). He considered that

as we in England have to transform our civilisation, so America has hers still to make; and that though her example and co-operation might, and probably would, be of the greatest value to us in the future, yet they were not of much use to our civilisation now. (Allott, 1953, p. 6)

The divinity of the average man as proclaimed by Whitman's *Leaves of Grass* (1854) offended many Englishmen: 'divine am I inside and out, and I make holy whatever I touch or am touched from . . . the scent of these armpits is aroma finer than prayer, this head is more than churches or bibles or creeds.' But some in the industrial North found in him, as their fathers found in Emerson, such an inspiration that they gathered in groups to discuss him. 'God bless the Church and branch of the Church (with candelabras blazing more fervidly than any), that is planted and grown in Bolton', wrote Walt Whitman to his 'Bolton College' on 28 July 1891. This 'College' was then six years old, composed of Lancashire business men who regularly gathered together as a kind of devotional group animated by a quasi-religious spirit (Blodgett, 1934). Just before his death he told them:

> more and more it comes to the fore that the only theory worthy of our modern times for g't literature politics and sociology must combine all the bulk—people of all lands the women not forgetting. (*T. L. S.*, 3 June 1918)

Such 'bulk-people' were the 'new men' of Victorian England. Some of them envied the opportunity offered by the transatlantic Eden to build things new after discarding old customs and burning old title deeds. Erosive criticism of the old English customs was provided by the American consul in Liverpool from 1853 to 1857 who suggested that by 1900 England would be a minor republic under the protection of the U.S. Sometimes he even thought the United States should annex Britain—a 'blood encrusted monarchical caste ridden power' (Wagenknecht, 1961, p. 117). He wrote the real parable of his times in *Earth's Holocaust* (1844). This told the story of a crowd of people gathered round a great prairie bonfire burning the world's 'outworn trumpery'. 'Now', said the chief incinerator, 'we shall get rid of the weight of dead men's thoughts.' This purgatorial action, as one recent commentator observes, preceded, 'as it were, the life of the new Adam in the new earthly paradise' (Lewis, 1955, p. 14).

This myth of America as the new earthly paradise, with all its offensive implications to the English tradition, had been previously and more perceptibly outlined by Fenimore Cooper:

All the familiar thoughts and illustrations of English

literature are in direct and dangerous opposition to our own system, and yet we are unwilling to support a writer in the promulgation of those that in harmony with our profession . . . It is manifestly to their interest to do our thinking, if possible, that they may do other things for us that are more lucrative; and they are not scrupulous about the means employed to effect this object. They systematically attack and undervalue every man they believe independent of their influence and extol those in the skies who will do their work. (Beard, 1960, ii. 38f)

Looking at England at first hand in 1832, Cooper wrote:

there probably never has been a period in the history of the nation, when the power of the few has been so indisputed in practice, or its exercise more under the sense of correction. (Spiller, 1936, p. 95)

The dominant image of the American as Adam, 'the first the archetype man' was the theme of all his Leatherstocking novels:—*The Pioneers* (1823); *The Pilot* (1823); *The Last of the Mohicans* (1826); *The Prairie* (1827); *The Red Rover* (1828); *The Wept of Wish-ton-Wish* (1829); and the *Water Witch* (1831). Best sellers over three decades, they exhaled an 'antinomian belief in primal perfection as well as progress towards perfection which caught the imagination and appealed to the inner needs of Englishmen'. For 'Adam was the first, the archetypal man'. His moral position was prior to experience and in his very newness he was fundamentally innocent. The world and history lay before him (Lewis, 1955, p. 5). This, as D. H. Lawrence felt, was 'the true myth of America. She starts old, wrinkled and writhing in an old skin. And there is a gradual sloughing off of the old skin towards a new youth. It is the myth of America' (Lewis, 1955, p. 103).

(iv)

Books carrying this myth poured so prodigally from American pens, that English railway station bookstalls contained more American than British books. The consequence made 'our different classes more intimate with American domestic life than they are with that of any other class among their countrymen beyond their own' (Monckton Milnes, 1876, p. 277). A more modern observer concluded that another result was that the British middle class became 'favourably disposed toward the United States. . . . And it certainly aided in the promulgation of liberal political views, for in the English sense of the word these popular American authors were all radicals' (Godhes, 1944, pp. 143–5).

Where cheap books could not get the message across, free libraries did. Even here, American influence was paramount. 'My own personal experience', wrote Andrew Carnegie, 'may have led me to value a free library beyond all forms of beneficence.' And Carnegie's beneficence, beginning at Dunfermline in 1881, spread to other towns in Britain and the U.S.A. At his death in 1919, he had enabled 2,505 library buildings to be built, costing $40 million in the United States and Canada alone. Of these, 380 buildings were in the United Kingdom, and if we include the Dominions, nearly 1,500 (Daniel, 1961, pp. 15–18).

These libraries themselves posed problems which the Americans were the first to appreciate. A small group of American librarians meeting at Philadelphia in 1876—the centennial celebration of Independence—decided to form the American Library Association, with Melvil Dewey as secretary. Attending this meeting was James Yeats, the librarian of Leeds Public Library, who was elected a vice-president. This Philadelphian meeting inspired Edward B. Nicholson to convene a similar group in London. Endorsed by *The Times* on 16 February 1877, it resulted in the formation of the English Library Association, a body which spread still further the technique developed by Melvil Dewey: the decimal system for classifying and cataloguing accessions (Hetherington, 1919, p. 84).

(v)

The American Eden was more operational than mythical. Secular parables on the need for constant vigilance and scrutiny to keep out the serpent created a regular literary type: the detective. Here Edgar Allen Poe provided a model in the pipe-smoking, moody Dupin, so admired by the English author, A. Conan Doyle. Doyle, in fact, christened his most famous character after another American, Oliver Wendell Holmes, whom he virtually worshipped: 'Never have I so known and loved a man whom I had never seen', he confessed. 'It was one of the ambitions of my lifetime to look upon his face, but by the irony of Fate I arrived in his native city just in time to lay a wreath upon his newly turned grave' (Pearson, 1946, pp. 19–20).

Though Conan Doyle confessed he sometimes wished he had never created Sherlock Holmes, since it prevented due appreciation being given to his historical novels, he nonetheless eagerly accepted the offer of the American actor William Gillette to put Holmes on the stage. By doing so, Gillette virtually created the image of Sherlock Holmes in his play of that name. His portrayal at the Star Theatre, Buffalo, on 23 October 1899 and later at the Garrick and Lyceum Theatres in London, virtually created the image as we know it with the deer-stalker cap over the lean, hungry face.

Though Conan Doyle identified himself with those who looked forward to an Anglo-American federation, he deplored the materialistic outlook of many Americans, complaining whilst in Pittsburgh that 'God sent a man into this world that he might improve in mind and spirit, and not that he should make screws and rivets' (Pearson, 1964, p. 191).

But screws and rivets were, as a superintendent of schools in Trenton, New Jersey, discovered, vital parts of the mechanical mystique of every American boy. His *The Steam Man of the Prairies* (1868) told the story of a fifteen-year-old mechanic who used the profits of his steam man to educate himself in order to build an even better man. The better man duly emerged, not from the brain of Edward Sylvester Ellis, but from the pages of *Boys of New York* in 1876. With steam men, steam horses, steam team and steam carriage, all in various ways instruments for taming the West, this better man, Frank Reade, was the fictional archetype of the mechanically-minded boy. Jules Verne picked up the idea for a serial of his own in an English boys' paper, *The Union Jack*, from 1880 to 1881.

Verne's admiration for American inventiveness had been already expressed in *From the Earth to the Moon* (1865). This told the story of a space craft to which every country in the world had contributed except the British, who received the plan with 'contemptuous apathy'. Verne's disciple, Hugo Gernsback, a technically trained European immigrant, popularised science fiction in the United States by writing 'Ralph 124C41 +' for his magazine *Modern Electrics* in 1911. This was so successful that he launched a special vehicle for others, *Amazing Stories*, and appointed Edison's son-in-law, Dr. T. O'Conor Sloane, to help select them. In yet a third magazine, *Science Wonder Stories*, Gernsback first used the term 'Science Fiction' (Moskowitz, 1963, p. 322).

Such fiction met a real social need in the America of the New Deal. *Amazing Stories* and *Wonder Stories* set a trend which was eagerly followed by others with titles like *Captain Future* and *Unknown*. Of these others the most significant was *Astounding Stories*. First appearing in 1930, it went through three changes of name and editors before becoming *Analog*. Its most dynamic editor,

John W. Campbell Jnr., made it a carrier of prophecy so accurate that the F.B.I. grilled him in 1944 for anticipating the fuse mechanism for the atomic bomb. Himself a predictive fantast under the name of Don. A. Stuart, Campbell coaxed predictive fantasy out of others, openly admitting to using his editorial power for 'subterranean education; to spread ideas which may help to break established patterns of thought'. Indeed, for this reason his magazine was nicknamed 'Monologue' (Williams, 1965). 'Technically,' he wrote, 'an *analog* is a system which behaves in a manner similar to some other and less manipulable system, so that it is easier and more convenient to study.' He saw science fiction as 'a convenient analog system for thinking about new scientific, social and economic ideas— and for examining old ideas' (Campbell, 1964). As a literary laboratory, its columns carried stories that later became novels. Such well-known writers as Robert Heinlein, A. E. van Vogt, Isaac Asimov, Theodore Sturgeon, Henry Kuttner and Catherine L. Moore used it as a test bed.

Other test beds were *The Magazine of Fantasy and Science*, where some of the best work of Richard Matheson, Ward Moore and Walter M. Miller was rehearsed; *Galaxy Science Fiction*, which carried Ray Bradbury's first novel, later known as *Fahrenheit 451*; Alfred Bester's *The Demolished Man*; Pohl and Kornbluth's *Gravy Planet*; and Isaac Asimov's *The Caves of Steel*.

(vi)

Such stories as these and others wrote transcended normal mechanistic and biological models, by adding a psychological dimension. Biologists and physicists tend to consider systems 'as developing societies of trends, in which each trend describes events in a collectivity without predicting the behaviour of the individual elements out of which the collectivity is made'. Science fiction aims at supplying the missing component.

One of the major sociological parables of this kind was *Brave New World* (1931). Its author, Aldous Huxley, as readers of another of his novels, *Antic Hay*, know, graduated from being a sub-editor on *House and Garden* to writing for *Vogue*, to which he regularly contributed till 1929. Both periodicals were owned by the American publisher, Condé Nast. This experience is easily recognisable in the polychromatic pictures of the 'Age of our Ford'.

Brilliantly exploited by such English writers as Olaf Stapledon, Eric Frank Russell, C. S. Lewis and George Orwell, as a medium for moral sermons, it is currently supplanting 'westerns' in the wire racks of paper-backs that, in American style, adorn newsagents' and chemists' shops. The 'neurosis of the future', which many of these science fiction stories embody, represents a retreat from the unbridled optimism of the American dream, and an undoubted reaction against the crude scientism that some see as America's most dangerous gift.

4
The Land Grant example

The cradles of this scientism were the land grant colleges, founded 'to teach such branches of learning as are related to agriculture and the mechanic arts', and to 'promote the liberal and practical education of the industrial classes in the several pursuits and professions of life'. Their charter was the Morrill Land Grant Act, passed in 1862, giving each state 30,000 acres of public land per representative and senator for building colleges in which such teaching could go forward.

The 'splendid scale' of these Federal appropriations moved the young English radical, Sir Charles Dilke. 'What has been done in the Eastern and Central States no man can tell,' he wrote in 1867, 'but even west of the Mississippi twenty-two million acres have already been granted for such purposes, while fifty-six million more are set aside for similar gifts' (Dilke, 1868, pp. 192–3).

Their aggressive practicality led Matthew Arnold to criticise them as 'calculated to produce miners, or engineers, or architects, not sweetness and light'. To him they were to be reckoned among 'the enemies' of culture, since they were founded 'on a miscalculation of what culture truly is' (Arnold, 1932, p. 22).

Arnold described the United States as 'up to the present

centres of extension teaching, and a Bureau of General Welfare. Dairymen saved hundreds of millions of dollars through the Babcock fat test. The progressive party employed professors to prepare their memoranda to such an extent that Madison was known as a University State rather than the site of a State University. The prospect first appalled, then enchanted, that shrewd English political commentator Goldsworthy Lowes Dickinson. At first, he found it 'the very antithesis' of his own university of Cambridge, since it helped the state 'to assess its taxes and value its property and even has a bureau of classified information for legislation'. 'I'm inclined to think,' he wrote, 'after all I've now seen here, that Oxford and Cambridge really are now the last refuges [of culture].'

He met three Canadians who confessed that the Americans had got us 'skinned alive in all application of science, but they know in their hearts that we have the one thing they won't get by all their efforts: disinterested intellectual culture'. Later, however, he discovered the American professors to be 'much more tolerant and free-minded than the similar herd in England. And they are human beings, which most of ours aren't.' And concluded: 'Perhaps after all I shall end my life in this country' (Forster, 1934, pp. 130, 168).

The Wisconsin concept of a community service station appealed to the newer English universities, too. A deputation from the University of Reading preferred another metaphor: that of 'a lever to be used in numerous ways to advance the interests of civilisation'. Having seen it at work, the Reading deputation noted that this led to far less hesitation about the propriety of liberal state aid.

The Reading report on *The Problems of Agricultural Education in England and America* (1910) coincided with an awakening interest exhibited by the English banker-sociologist, Victor Branford, and his friend, Patrick Geddes, who devoted their lives to improving the inter-action of the university and the region. Geddes especially wanted, as he said, 'to avoid the separation of the school of industry from the school of science, which produces pedants in the university and philistines in the workshop' (Branford, 1914, pp. 33–6). Both Geddes and Branford owed much to another American, Charles Ferguson, whose *University Militant* (1911) and concept of Technarchy (the age of the engineers) they were to humanise.

The Wisconsin pattern continued to attract the British left, always anxious to promote the intellectual in politics. Thus a Labour M.P. saw it as 'on many counts the most interesting state in the Union', where politics 'enlist the active co-operation and concern of the intellectuals and excite the ardent interest of citizens of all kinds. There the University and the State Capitol work closely hand in hand' (Hamilton, 1932). She attended one of John R. Common's weekly suppers at Madison and found it a 'most alive and human centre'.

(iii)

Land grants apart, higher education in the United States continued to expand through demand from below. A scheme to train Sunday School teachers, begun in 1874 by the side of Lake Chautauqua as a summer school, became in ten years a peripatetic university, empowered by the State of New York to award its own degrees.

By concentrating only on summer courses, Chautauqua was unique. No other university in the world was so efficiently run by part-time teachers. Its literary and scientific circles, its schools of pedagogy, languages and theology, were all staffed by men with full-time appointments elsewhere, and even the Principal of its College of Liberal Arts from 1887 to 1898, William Rainey Harper, was a teacher first at Denison College in Ohio and later at the Union Theological Seminary at Morgan Park, Illinois.

Chautauqua was, in the eyes of its founder, J. H. Vincent,

'a John the Baptist, preparing the way for seminary and university'. To quote him again,

> College life is the whole of life packed into a brief period, with the elements that make life magnified and intensified, so that tests of character can easily be made. It is a laboratory of experiment, where natural laws and conditions are pressed into rapid though normal operation, and processes otherwise extending over long periods of time are crowded to speedy consummation. . . . Argument should be used, appeals made, assistance preferred, that a larger percentage of American youth may aspire after college privileges. . . . Chautauqua lifts up its voice in favour of liberal education for a larger number of people. (Gould, 1961, pp. 22, 60)

This concept of universalised college education appealed to the Baptists, who dreamt of a super-university in New York, founded and sustained by their wealthiest supporter, John D. Rockefeller. Rockefeller turned down the idea of founding one in New York, but leant strongly to William Rainey Harper's scheme for building it round a small Baptist college in Chicago.

So on an initial endowment of two million dollars from Rockefeller and a charter from the State of Illinois, in 1890 the University of Chicago opened its doors under William Rainey Harper as President. This carried the concept of universalised college education a step further, since to the university proper was now added extension and publication. In the academies, colleges, affiliated colleges and schools, the year's work was to be organised in four quarters, each of two six-week terms, enabling students to enter or graduate on any one of eight dates during the regular school year. Each student was to take a 'major' of twelve hours' classroom work each week, and a 'minor' of six.

The organisation of Chautauqua, proposed by Dr. Vincent

to his trustees six years earlier, was the blueprint of the constitution of Chicago as proposed by William Rainey Harper in 1891. Harper emphasised continuous sessions, concentrated periods of study, correspondence teaching, examination and publication.

Visiting it fifteen years later, H. G. Wells found it the equivalent of Harvard and Columbia:

> each in its material embodiment already larger, wealthier and more hopeful than any contemporary British institutions and much more conscious of their role in the future of their country: intelligently antagonist to lethargic and self-indulgent traditions. . . . It is from them that the deliberate invasion of the political machine by independent men of honour and position proceed. (Wells, 1906, pp. 302–3).

(iv)

The impact of all this on new and struggling universities in the English industrial towns was direct and immediate. 'I fear none of Mason College buildings and not much of its apparatus would be of the slightest use as part of a modern scientific university school', Andrew Carnegie told Joseph Chamberlain, then chairman of the Mason College council. So Chamberlain sent his friend, G. H. Kenrick, and two of the Professors of the College to the United States and Canada in the autumn of 1899. 'Not until after this visit to America', wrote the historians of what soon became the University of Birmingham, 'did the committee arrive at some conception of what was required of them.' That conception involved securing a site outside the town at Edgbaston, and pressing ahead for a charter. Chamberlain acknowledged that the report of the deputation to America

> opened my eyes and I think it must have opened the

eyes of all who have read it. The Committee found great institutions connected with a general university, real colleges of Science occupying large spaces, in which the area was counted by many acres, fully equipped with proper buildings with the most modern and complete machinery, with the latest scientific purpose. And in these great colleges a training was given such as we desire to see imitated in this country, a training based, as all education ought to be, upon a foundation of general culture, but specialised according to the work which each student intends to take in life. And as a result of this we begin to see how it is that in America the great commercial and industrial undertakings . . . found no difficulty whatever in obtaining the services of as many young men as they may require to manage and complete and develop the undertakings. (Vincent and Hinton, 1947, pp. 28, 34)

Chamberlain imported from Harvard a Professor of Economics, W. J. Ashley, to get the Social Sciences under way, and soon Birmingham was setting a pace which the other civic colleges followed by supplicating for charters.

(v)

Oxford also followed suit, by bringing over William Osler to its Regius Chair of Medicine in 1904. From here, he worked for the introduction of hospital units in London, serving on the Royal Commission on the University of London in 1910, as well as on the Welsh University Commission in 1916 during the first World War, when he can be credited with responsibility for the proposal that a National School of Medicine should be created at Cardiff.

Osler's work was in the tradition of the University from which he came, Johns Hopkins, at Baltimore. This was a post-graduate university and medical school opened in 1876 as a result of the generosity of Johns Hopkins, a Baltimore merchant. Osler was its first professor of medicine and William Welch its first professor of physiology.

Welch brought to Baltimore the European habit of using the methods of fundamental science in medical schools, and he persuaded Frederick T. Gates, Rockefeller's 'particular Baptist minister', to draft a memorandum to that great philanthropist out of which emerged the Rockefeller Institute for Medical Research. This began functioning in 1904 under Simon Flexner, one of Welch's pupils, as first director. In 1906, the institute moved to the banks of the East River in New York City, and in 1910 a research hospital, the first of its kind in America, was added.

Unlike European institutes (the Pasteur Institute in Paris, or the Imperial Health Office in Berlin), which were built around one man, the Rockefeller Institute was built about problems. So whereas they emphasised bacteriology and immunology, it included biology, physics and chemistry. Dr. Flexner had learned from Welch that the important medical advances of the future would come from basic science. And Johns Hopkins, as we shall see, was to present yet another facet of that ever-changing institution, the university, to the English for yet further emulation.

(vi)

Oxford's general reaction to American influence might be gauged from George Calderon's novel *The Adventures of Downy V. Green, Rhodes Scholar at Oxford* (1902). Based on one of the most famous books on English University life—Edward Bradley's *The Adventures of Mr Verdant Green* (1854–57)—it told the story of Verdant Green's grandson, an American at Oxford (Verdant Green's son having emigrated to America and made his fortune in soap).

A very real American soap magnate was, in fact, extremely active in England at this time: Joseph Fels. He was in the great tradition of American philanthropists in England, like George Peabody (who financed housing projects in mid-nineteenth century London) and Andrew Carnegie (whose trusts were to do so much for the unemployed in the twentieth). Fels brought 1,300 acres of land at Hollesley Bay for the unemployed, financed the first health centres and backed Keir Hardie and George Lansbury. The labour cause in Britain was yet further helped by another wealthy American at Oxford, Walter Vrooman, who with a fellow American, Charles Beard, founded Ruskin College. Ruskin College was to provide a small but effective recuperator mechanism for working class men of ability to enjoy a university education.

Other representatives of the world of labour, twenty-three to be exact, were sent to America in 1903 by Alfred Mosely, who had, whilst in South Africa, came to appreciate the work of American mining engineers who so successfully built bridges for the British Army during the Boer War. These representatives reported that

One of the principal reasons why the American workman is better than the Britisher is that he has received a senior and better education, whereby he has been more thoroughly fitted for the struggles of after life.

We are satisfied that, in the years to come, in competing with American commerce we shall be called upon to face trained men, gifted with both enterprise and knowledge. We desire to impress on the British public the absolute need of immediate preparation on our part to meet such competition. (Mosely, 1903)

At the same time Mosely sent twenty-five representatives of the educational world to America, including the President of the National Union of Teachers. The tone of their findings was perhaps best summarised by a book,

Education and Industrial Success (1904) written by a member of this group, W. P. Groser.

Perhaps the strangest detonation took place in public schools. H. B. Gray, the Warden of Bradfield, perhaps best known for his initiation of open-air Greek plays (in a disused quarry near the school), found service on the Mosely educational commission in 1903 to be a journey to Damascus, and put on record that the teaching of English in America was 'remarkably good, and far outstrips anything of which we can boast', whilst the 'teaching of science in all its branches appeared admirable'. So impressed was he by American schools and curricula that, after his retirement from Bradfield in 1910, he devoted the rest of his active and energetic life to a spirited campaign against the caste nature and didactic system of English public schools. His was the bitterest and most thorough criticism which English public schools had yet received from one who knew them as a responsible person. It was a plea for a flexible and original curriculum based on observation of men and nature. Public schools, in his view, should not aim at producing prancing proconsuls and rulers of inferior peoples, but participants in a co-operating commonwealth.

Mosely was also responsible for initiating in 1906–7 the visit of several hundred school-children to the United States and Canada, a project first mooted by Choate, the U.S. Ambassador, in 1901. In 1909, the then Vice-Chancellor of Sheffield conceived the notion that a twentieth-century 'grand tour' should embrace the New World, and a movement was set on foot to promote it. In 1910, the Central Bureau for the International Exchange of Students opened to increase our 'efficiency as citizens'.

Mosely's initiative was followed by the newly-created local authorities, eleven of whose representatives had travelled with his educational party to America in 1903. The districts they represented were important ones: London, the West Riding, Newcastle, Sheffield, Liverpool, Manchester and Rochdale.

Other authorities, which had not been represented on it, soon took steps to remedy their deficiencies in this respect. Leicester sent a deputation which reported in 1907. Reading (backed by L. Sutton, the seed merchant, and Alfred Palmer, the biscuit manufacturer) sent a fact-finding group to examine American agricultural colleges which reported in 1910. The permanent officials of the authorities, whom we would now refer to as their directors of education, sent a deputation of their own in 1911 to examine technical schools, and this report, compiled by the secretaries of the Barnsley, Ealing, West Bromwich and St. Helens authorities, was warm in its praise of American vocational schools as compared to English ones. Local authorities so primed themselves with information about technical schools and colleges in America that when, in 1918, they were empowered to levy more than a twopenny rate to finance such colleges, they went ahead, prodded by the various professional associations, to emulate what they had seen.

Academic traffic to America was further facilitated by a former member of Lord Northcliffe's staff, Sir Evelyn Wrench, who in 1906 founded the Overseas Club, later the Overseas League. After the first World War he and the American ambassador, Walter Hines Page, founded the English-Speaking Union, which absorbed the oldest of the Anglo-American voluntary societies (founded in 1897 by Sir Walter Besant, another journalist of similar sympathies). Wrench not only served both societies in an administrative capacity, but, as editor of *The Spectator* from 1925 to 1932 extended the hospitality of its pages to interpreters of the American tradition.

5

The twentieth century university

English awareness of the academic explosion in America
slowly changed to apprehension. Two years before he
became British ambassador in Washington, James Bryce
observed that 'within these last thirty-five years' there
had been 'a development of the higher education in the
United States perhaps without parallel in the world'.
'Even more noticeable', he continued, 'is the amplitude of
the provision now made for the study of the natural
sciences and of those arts in which science is applied to
practical ends. In this respect the United States has gone
ahead of Great Britain' (Bryce, 1905; Nevins, 1948, p. 389).
After visiting the U.S.A. during the first World War, A. J.
Balfour hoped to attract American post-graduate students
to Britain, but was defeated by the anarchic autonomy of
British universities. He lamented their

> lack of any common organisation or meeting ground
> for consultation, which made it very difficult for
> Americans who might desire to finish their studies
> abroad to find out what work was being done in Great
> Britain and what university could best provide for their
> needs. (Ashby, 1963, p. 19)

The 'lack of any common organisation' was remedied by the establishment a year later of a 'standing conference' of Vice-Chancellors and Universities, or, as it was later known, the Committee of Vice-Chancellors and Principals.

Two innovations followed from the American invasion of Oxford: the establishment of the D. Phil. (or the Ph.D. as it is known in other universities), and the abolition of compulsory Greek. The latter, a result of difficulties with the Rhodes scholars, had corresponding repercussions in the schools (Allen, 1944).

But instead of American students coming to England for post-graduate work, a trickle, increasing to a steady stream, of the best English graduates began to flow to America, helped from 1925 onwards, by the Common-wealth Fund, established by Mrs. Harkness in 1916 to sub-sidise young men and women 'of character and ability' to come to the U.S.A. for study and travel. No less than 411 such fellowships had been awarded up to 1940, and by 1956, over 300 of them were engaged in academic work. It was said that

> if all of the fellows so engaged could have been assembled on one campus, they would have constituted a university faculty of respectable size, including all departments, some of them particularly strong.
>
> (Commonwealth Fund, 1963, p. 85)

Another such fellowship programme was provided by the Rockefeller Foundation. Begun during the first World War, several hundred fellowships were soon being awarded annually in the Medical, Natural and Social Sciences, the Humanities and the Public Health. By 1950, 6,342 fellowships had been awarded to seventy-five coun-tries. So the current which Balfour hoped would flow to England set in the reverse direction. This westward drift of English graduate students was due to the obviously superior resources of American universities. Even in 1940, nine individual American universities enjoyed an annual income greater than the total Parliamentary grant to all British universities, a sum also surpassed by five states of the Union in their own grants to universities.

(ii)

'Those of us who had not hitherto had the privilege of visiting the United States', said the Vice-Chancellor of Cambridge in 1918, after visiting America as a member of the British University Mission, 'formed the idea that all its cities are university cities and that all the inhabitants are professors' (Shipley, 1919).

Indeed, the failure of the whole European system of higher education was sensitively and humanely deplored in that year by Henry Adams, a former Harvard professor. After being previously circulated to his friends, *The Education of Henry Adams* (1918) evoked widespread discussion. For Adams really argued for a complete reassessment of all the elements that go to educating for maturity. Convinced that the principles of freedom were being perpetually converted to the principles of power, that the worship of the Virgin was now supplanted by the worship of the Dynamo, that science and its principles must form an integral part of culture, Adams presented his report in the third person, giving it a tartness and objectivity that made for better reading.

Further cartographical information about the American approach to the *speculum mentis* was provided by Abraham Flexner. 'A university professor has an entirely objective responsibility to learning,' he wrote, 'to his subject, and not a psychological or parental responsibility to his students'. To him, the most important function of a university was the intensive study of phenomena under the most favourable conditions.

He insisted that the specialist was needed in the modern world, not men content with half-knowledge. 'However deeply the flash of genius may penetrate,' Flexner insisted, 'the bulk of the world's research and teaching will be done in universities—if universities are what they should be' (Flexner, 1930, p. 20). That Flexner could so magisterially survey universities in England and Germany as well as in his own country, and that his book should be taken so seriously itself, indicated how important American precedent had become. Flexner acknowledged that his concept of a university was 'severe' and that he might give the impression that he was 'really discussing institutes of research rather than universities'. But on one aspect of English university development he was clear—its financing was indeed poor.

(iii)

Poor but proud, the British treasury didn't much approve of charity. 'We do not want the British Government', Sir Winston Churchill told Sir William Beveridge, 'to be mixed up with what I may call coaxing and wheedling cash out of the United States' (Beveridge, 1953, p. 195). As Chancellor of the Exchequer in 1926 Churchill refused to help the University of London acquire a central headquarters in 1926, either by a grant or by supporting a request to the Rockefeller trust. So, after coaxing and wheedling on his own, Beveridge was given £400,000 from the Rockefeller Trust to help purchase the Bloomsbury site. Here a white functional central headquarters was built, rising above the congeries of academic buildings in the Bloomsbury ideopolis which stands today as a monument to American charity.

Nor is it the only one in London. For in the same year, Beveridge's own London School of Economics obtained the wherewithal (some £180,000) to foster the Social Sciences, whilst earlier, the University College Hospital Medical School was given £835,000, also by the Rockefeller Trust, to enable it to remodel itself on American lines with full-time clinical teachers.

Supplications for Rockefeller grants to remodel the long

outdated library accommodation at both Cambridge and Oxford were also successful. The need at Cambridge had been manifest since the seventeenth century, and neither the conversion of the old Senate House in the eighteenth, nor a series of extensions in the nineteenth century, could mask it. Seven and a half acres of land were obtained from King's and Clare, and Giles Gilbert Scott submitted plans for a new library costing half a million pounds. Half of this came from the Rockefeller Education Board. The Board did more! They invited a commission to visit some of the chief American libraries, a visit which was undertaken in the autumn of 1930. In gratitude, the University named the main reading room in the South Pavilion after Sir Hugh Kerr Anderson, the Master of Caius, to whom 'more than any other man' was due the securing of the Rockefeller grant.

One Oxford scheme (which included rooms for advanced study and research) was defeated by a large majority before Congregation, and another, for a store on the Broad Street site, was also defeated on the same day. Here the Rockefeller Foundation slipped in and suggested that they should make official enquiries at other newly-constructed libraries in Europe and America. This the University accepted on 4 March 1930, appointing Sir Henry Miers as chairman of a commission, which issued a long report, *Library Provision in Oxford* (1931), a modified version of the second Scheme and estimated to cost £944,300. The Rockefeller Trustees agreed to contribute three-fifths of this on condition that the University found the remaining two-fifths within a given period of four and a half years. That condition was satisfied in one (Fosdick, 1952, pp. 263–4).

Other venerable British institutions were helped by the Pilgrim Trust, also founded in 1930 by Edward S. Harkness. Administered by British trustees, this made grants to St. Andrews University and to the Shakespeare Memorial Theatre at Stratford-on-Avon. Ironically, it helped keep alive the very institutions which cosseted old English traditions, even though such traditions were, as we have seen, being vigorously challenged by America.

(iv)

One of the most imperative challenges was to the specialist undergraduate curriculum as it was understood in England. For as the specialist core of American education moved up to the graduate schools—whose population grew from 5,668 in 1900 to 223,786 in 1950—new courses were tried at college level. These were based either on full study of an ancient civilisation and a modern one, as developed from 1926 to 1933 by Alexander Meiklejohn at the University of Wisconsin, or on 'great books', a course developed by John Erskine, Mortimer J. Adler and Mark van Doren, at Chicago, and at St. John's College in Maryland.

Both experiments caught the interest of F. R. Leavis at Cambridge, then bent on beaming his own ideas towards the sixth forms, the English equivalent of the American junior college. These ideas, to be embodied in *Culture and Environment* (1933), were almost specifically levelled at the American elements in modern life—Mass Production, Advertising, Levelling Down, the Supply of Reading Matter, the Use of Leisure, Tradition, Substitute Living, Education and the Business Ethos.

In the first volume of his increasingly influential quarterly *Scrutiny*, Leavis commented on Meiklejohn's 'immediate relevance' to that journal's aims and advised readers 'in the strongest terms' to 'correct the injustice it inevitably suffers here' by reading his account of it in *The Experimental College* (1932).

The true tribute to Dr. Meiklejohn and his colleagues would be to suggest how the spirit, and, to a great extent, the technique, of the Experimental College might be applied in a real training of intelligence, and be always associated with the training of sensibility in the literature of the student's own language.

(Scrutiny, i (1933), 299–30)

Leavis was also much seized of Brooks Otis' 'admirable theoretical statement' that 'our present educational problem is to devise a method of "cultural instruction" which will—in the modern world—take the place of the old "liberal arts" ', and expressed a hope that 'something might be made of the English Tripos' (*Scrutiny*, ii (1930), 333).

After laying down his own canon of 'great books' Leavis crystallised his ideas in *Education and the University* (1943), where he paid tribute to Ezra Pound 'for saying in a concise and challenging way some things that seemed to me to need saying'. These ideas were for a course based on the transformation of seventeenth century England into the England of today. At the same time, his associate L. C. Knights published an essay on Bacon's *Novum Organum* calling attention to the symbol on the title page:

a ship in full sail, setting out beyond the Pillars of Hercules towards the new and uncharted lands. Today, [concluded Knights]—in 'this American world' of scientific progress—the symbol is seen to have been specially appropriate.

(Scrutiny, iii (1935), 122–3)

(v)

'There is nothing, however fantastic, that (given competent organisation), a team of engineers, scientists and administrators cannot do today.' So David Lilienthal of the Tennessee Valley Authority and later of the Atomic Energy Commission outlined the American faith : 'a philosophy and a set of working tools [to] guide and sustain us in increasing opportunity for individual freedom' (Lilienthal, 1944, p. 3).

The result of this faith, as Ramsay Muir acknowledged, was that American industry had, over the greater part of its range, 'accepted the methods of science and pinned its faith to research and enquiry, in a degree not equalled in any modern country'. 'I believe', Ramsay Muir continued, 'that the main cause is to be found in the very wide diffusion of higher or university education.' This diffusion was such that America, with less than three times the population of Britain, had more than twenty times as many university students. So a college education for children had become a 'normal duty for all middle class parents and attainable ambition of the working classes'.

Two profound social consequences flowed from this: 'a vast army of trained investigators' was produced for the research mechanisms of American industry, whilst 'a notion of what scientific and objective methods of inquiry really mean' was widely diffused. As Muir wisely concluded,

> Even if the crowds who pass through the universities get no more than this, they do get this, and they take into every walk of life a readiness to submit every puzzling problem to scientific investigation, and a knowledge that there are men who make it their business to do this kind of work.

> (Muir, 1927, pp. 31–2)

That American universities nourished more than mere expertise needs no elaboration. To George Santayana, 'to be an American is of itself almost a moral condition, an education and a career' (1920, p. 168). To Logan Pearsall Smith, Americans acted 'as if America were more than a country, were a sort of cause' (1939, p. 280).

Even the sensitive Unitarian L. P. Jacks, returning to the scene he had known as a student fifty years before, was astonished at the technical 'intelligentsia' which had

57

grown up in the interval. Their organised systems of recreation, their constant debates and their employment of play and creative energy in teaching much impressed him.

the whole country might be described as one vast poly-technic; perhaps 'polytechnic civilisation' would be a better name than 'industrial civilisation' for the stage of evolution through which America is now passing with all the western world at her heels. Technique, always in process of further refinement, has imposed herself on everything, invading not only the world of material objects but the world of human relations, where it has become established under the name of 'psychology'.

(Nevins, 1945, p. 415)

Here, as in so many other fields, H. G. Wells seemed to have not so much the last as the first word. Descanting, in one of his inter-war satires, on the difficulty of absorbing modern industrial and commercial subjects into British universities, one of his characters exclaims :

Birth-rates and emigration and statistics. An invasion of laborious clap-trap on an unprecedented scale [the master reiterated]. Laborious clap-trap. We had better import a few Americans to show us how.

(Wells, 1937, p. 4)

The impact of American culture on the rest of the world had, in the opinion of a Labour Peer, 'something of the force of a compulsive neurosis, to question any part of it is to set one's face against the light'. He continued:

The American firms which are now entering British and other markets in increasing numbers are doing some-thing much more effective than preaching a way of life —they are selling one.

(Williams, 1962, p. 47)

By 1963 this American 'intelligentsia' had grown so rapidly that C. P. Snow 'marvelled' at its 'astonishing' size. From St. Louis, Missouri, on 23 February 1963, he looked at the University of California and exclaimed:

There is nothing like that concentration of talent any-where in the world. It sometimes surprises Europeans to realize how much of the pure science of the entire West is being carried out in the United States. Curiously enough, it often surprises Americans too. At a guess, the figure is something like 60 per cent, and might easily be higher

(Kerr, 1964, pp. 92–3)

(vi)

After the second World War, the University Grants Committee, armed in 1946 with revised terms of reference to secure any 'development that might from time to time be required in order to ensure that universities were fully adequate to national needs', began to consider the possi-bility of 'building up one or more institutions of univer-sity rank devoted predominantly to the teaching and study of the various forms of technology'. And their avowed model in this was Massachusetts Institute of Tech-nology, which they had been visiting since the end of the war (Cmnd 8473, 1952, p. 60).

Consulted in 1953 with regard to the application of 9 million dollars allotted by the United States Government to the United Kingdom to promote the productivity of in-dustry in various countries, the U.G.C. recommended it to be used, amongst other things, for endowing three chairs or readerships at Imperial College (heavy, electrical and production engineering), one at Cambridge (in industrial management), and one at the Royal College of Science and Technology (in industrial management). That the filling of these posts proved so difficult was an indication of how new these subjects were in the British university world. The

U.G.C. confessed that it was 'symptomatic of the prevailing uncertainty about what should be the content of management studies as a distinctive university discipline' (Cmnd 534, 1958, p. 59).

The Anglo-American Productivity Team on Universities and Industry (1951) had first pointed to the need for more technologists at first degree level. Even assuming that the American first degree (B.S.) was the equivalent of the British Higher National Certificate, the team found that at this level America was producing three times as many engineers per head of population and a similar superiority at higher levels in the output of scientists. Taken up by the Parliamentary Scientific Committee, this resulted in the issue of the white paper on Technical Education, in which American figures of Russian advances were quoted

By 1960, just over a third of the age group in the U.S.A. were going to college, and British concern over the development of its own system of higher education was such that the Prime Minister set up a committee in 1960 under Lord Robbins to sketch its future pattern. This committee spent as much time in the U.S.A. as in all the other countries they visited taken together—except Russia—as well as talking to the president of M.I.T. in London. It called attention to the concentration of post-graduate work in the universities and the establishment of junior colleges for coping with the first two years of the under-graduate course. Their admiration for the former led them to recommend that five or six Special Institutions for Scientific and Technological Research should be established in Britain. The latter, especially in California, impressed them.

> Other states [it prophesied] may later have to adopt California's methods of planning; but they are a clean break with American tradition, in which all subjects of study and all institutions are treated alike and left to find their own level.

> (Cmd 2154, 1963, p. 37)

Appearing at a time when the 'brain drain' to America was exciting popular attention, the Robbins Report recommended the expansion of British universities, the broadening of their curricula on American models, and the establishment of schools and colleges of education.

The subsequent expansion of degrees which brought into the forward echelons of university life not only subjects like education, but marketing, business administration, and nursing, showed how seriously the American exemplar was being taken.

(vii)

American Universities were most effectively projected in England through the numerous exchange schemes operated not only by individual Universities but by organised programmes. Of the latter the most notable took its name from a former American Rhodes scholar at Oxford, Senator J. W. Fulbright, himself a former president of an American University. He hit on the idea of authorising the Department of State to use moneys from the sale of surplus war material in foreign countries to finance 'studies, research, instruction, and other educational activities of, or for, American colleges in those countries' or of the citizens of such countries in American educational institutions. From its inception after the war to 1962 the Fulbright scheme aided the exchange between the U.S.A. and the U.K. of nearly 9,000 teachers and scholars (4,087 U.S. and 4,952 U.K.). It also fostered conservation programmes in emergent African countries under British tutelage. Indeed, one quarter of the resources allocated to the U.K. went to Africa, enabling British biologists to participate in, amongst other things, the conservation of the great game herds and inspired the creation of the Nuffield Unit for Tropical Africa (Johnson and Colligan, 1965, p. 183).

Fulbright and the schemes that followed brought home to Englishmen the value of one of the most significant post-war developments in under-graduate teaching, that of the 'open University'. For not only had 569 school districts in America adopted open-circuit telecasting by 1960 but 117 colleges and Universities had done so as well. This 'University of the air' began in Chicago, where courses earning credit were broadcast from the educational station T.T.T.W. backed by the Fund for the Advancement of Education and the Chicago Board of Education. This was accompanied by closed circuit television at Pennsylvania State University, the University of Texas and Ohio State where increased numbers made imperative the more efficient use of space. In higher education television assumes 'almost entire obligation for the instruction of the student, who does not attend classes but views the programs and pursues his studies at home' (Gross and Murphy, 1964, p. 136). National commercial networks have caught on and have had thousands enrolled in credit-earning courses provided by 'Sunrise Semester'.

In Britain the idea caught on in 1964 when the Labour party, faced with similar pressures of numbers, put forward its idea for a 'University of the Air'. For in addition to developing another degree-earning group of colleges to the Universities, described by Mr. Crosland as the 'public sector', they added a third— the 'open University', based on television and correspondence courses. Originally conceived of as a 'University of the air' it was redesignated by the Minister for the Arts, as the person charged with its implementation, in a speech on 14 May 1966.

At the other end of the academic spectrum, new colleges at Oxford have been substantially helped by American money, whilst in between, at the large federal and civic universities, modified versions of the credit system of courses, long found necessary in American universities of similar size, are finding increasing favour.

6

The educational process

Education by means of direct contact with the environment was a by-product of rapid American expansion, so it was natural enough that Americans should appropriate and incorporate Pestalozzian ideas. From 1809 when Joseph Neef established the first Pestalozzian school at Philadelphia such ideas took vigorous root and flowered fourteen years later in a teacher-training institute at Concord, Vermont and others in New York (1827), and Massachusetts (1839) (Munroe, 1907). The American Institute of Instruction (1830) excited an English teacher to suggest a non-denominational teachers' union in 1853: an ideal not realised till 1870 with the founding of the N.U.T. (Tropp, 1957, p. 55).

These American teachers established journals. First *The Juvenile Monitor or Educational Magazine*, began in 1811, then the *Academician* in 1826. The latter was not only Pestalozzian but took its toll of all European journals and experiments. Others followed, like the *American Annals of Education* from which the *English Quarterly Journal of Education* 'had the habit of extracting entire articles' (Godhes, 1944, p. 53).

When Henry Barnard established the *American Journal of Education* in 1855 it was ruthlessly pillaged by English educationists. 'England has as yet nothing in the same field worthy of comparison with it', wrote the *Westminster Review* whilst Oscar Browning described it as 'by far the most valuable work in our language on the history of Education'. Indeed one of the latter's colleagues, on hearing that the plates of the journal would have to be melted down to meet expenses, declared that he 'would as soon hear that there was talk of pulling down one of our cathedrals and selling the stone for building material: all the best students use the *American Journal of Education*, or papers excerpted from it' (Thursfield, 1945, pp. 292, 299). This colleague, R. H. Quick, an early lecturer in education at Cambridge, himself published material from Barnard's numbers in the *British Monthly Journal of Education*.

(ii)

Amongst the pioneer journals carrying articles on the education of women was *The Lily*, the first paper of any kind published by a woman. It ran for six years, carrying vigorous articles on education, unjust marriage laws, and women's suffrage.

For the American woman kept pace with the American man, finding it easier to obtain a post in the professions or in industry than did her counterparts in any country in Europe. One visible sign of her emancipation was the sporting of the Bloomer costume. This, a bodice, short skirt and full trousers gathered in at the ankle, was promoted by Amelia Jenks Bloomer.

Just another such American, Elizabeth Blackwell, was an agent in extending professional opportunities to women in England. After graduating at Geneva Medical School, New York, she lost an eye whilst working in the obstetrical ward of a Paris hospital. Coming to St. Bartholomew's Hospital, London, in 1850 she practised every aspect of medicine, except, ironically, gynaecology and

pediatrics. She returned again nineteen years later to de-
vote herself to securing the free and equal entrance of
women to medical schools, becoming in 1875 Professor of
Gynaecology in the London School of Medicine for
Women, itself founded by one of her former students,
Sophia Jex-Blake. (O. R. MacGregor, 1955.)

Few Victorians took such women seriously. Gilbert and
Sullivan's *Princess Ida*, first performed at the Savoy
Theatre on 5 January 1884, caught the average English-
man's contempt for

A woman's college! maddest folly going!
What can girls learn within its walls worth knowing?
I'll lay a crown (the Princess shall decide it)
I'll teach them twice as much in half-an-hour outside it.

'High intellectual pressure', as Oscar Wilde's Lady
Markby remarked, was 'a most unbecoming thing' as it
made 'the noses of the young girls so particularly large'.
By the time Meredith had written *Lord Ormont and his
Aminta* (1894) co-education was coming in, 'partly',
according to a distinguished British historian of education,
'owing to the influence of America, whose early public
schools for the most obvious reasons taught boys and girls
in common' (Adamson, 1930, p. 461).

(iii)

It was an American also who pioneered a more rational
form of physical education for girls in English schools.
Moses Coit Tyler, coming to England in 1863, was invited to explain his system of eurhythmics, and encouraged to found the London School of Physical Education.
His eurhythmics claimed to 'rise far above the dreary
level of task-work and monotonous drudgery, and are
literally and permanently a pleasure. They recognise the
artistic necessity of touching the play-impulse. They

attempt to inaugurate, during the hour devoted to gymnastics, a sort of physical jubilee, a carnival of the emotional and vital powers' (Jones, 1933, p. 20). For whereas military gymnastics required poles, bars, vaulting horses, rings and ladders, to say nothing of drill sergeants, Tyler's simple eurhythmics could be adapted for girls and for the lower classes of the large towns, the very people upon whose fitness the nation depended. It was for this reason that he was invited to give evidence to the Schools Inquiry Commission in 1866. (Vol. VII, Appendix xiii, 587ff.)

Other new means of recreating the tired urban soul were created in America and exported. Baseball, curiously enough, was first professionalised by an English cricketer, Henry Wright, who brought over his team, Cincinnati, to England in 1874 to play certain cricket teams, a gesture which did much to democratise that traditional English game by stimulating the formation of various leagues. One of Wright's players, A. G. Spalding, pioneered the mass production of sporting equipment, and in turn also organised a baseball tour of England in 1888. The event survives in the name of the home ground of one of our leading professional football teams.

To keep players fit between the football and the baseball season, basketball was devised by Luther H. Gulick in 1891. This, the only major sport of wholly American origin, was cradled in the Y.M.C.A. training school at Springfield, Massachusetts (for which Gulick devised the red triangle, later to be adopted as the movement's sign). It took its name from the placing of two peach baskets ten feet high at either end of the running track. With its variant, netball, the game spread rapidly in England, especially when played by American soldiers.

The oldest organised sport in America, lacrosse, was played before Columbus' time by the Iroquois in upper New York and lower Ontario as a preparation for war, but by the nineteenth century had become widely popular as the fastest game on two feet. Following a visit of Indians to Britain, the English Lacrosse Association was formed in 1868. By 1882, the 'North' v. 'South' matches began. By 1897, a North of England League was formed, and by 1903 Oxford and Cambridge took it up (Krout, 1929).

For even in eclipse, the Indians influenced the English boy. As a result of Ernest Thompson Seton's book *How to Play Injun*, groups of American boys began to form, calling themselves 'Seton's Indians' or 'Woodcraft Indians' When Seton came to England on a lecture tour in 1904 and 1906, he sent a revised fifth edition of his *How to Play Injun*—this time retitled as *The Birch-bark Roll of the Woodcraft Indians*—to such English workers with boys' movements as might be interested, and one of them, General Baden-Powell, was to modify his own concepts of scouting. After hearing of Seton's Woodcraft Indians he noted in his diary:

Each 'camp' ruled by its own council. Each boy begins with a scalp which he loses if he fails to do something —and can only redeem by payment. He gains feathers and books by qualifying in various subjects (all out-door)—no competition, only qualifying. Scouting practices good.

These practices he successfully proved a year later in a test camp on Brownsea Island, the prelude to launching the Boy Scout Movement. In this test run, games from Seton's *Birch-bark Roll* were, by Baden-Powell's own admission, 'cribbed' (Hillcourt, 1964, pp. 257, 270). Seton subsequently became Chief Scout of America and as such received Baden-Powell in New York in 1910.

(iv)

For America lived vividly for the present. As Emerson wrote,

The question, whether one generation of men has a right to bind another, seems never to have started on this or our side of the water. Yet it is a question of such consequence as not only to merit decision, but place, also, among the fundamental principles of government . . . and set out on this ground which I suppose to be self-evident *'that the earth belongs in usufruct to the living;* that the dead have neither power nor right over it'.

(Lewis, 1955, pp. 16, 19)

This was congenial doctrine for reformers. Mere birth and traditional ways had such a small place in it. Even an English Emersonian like G. S. Venables could lament: 'Perhaps an American England may produce a higher average of happiness than the existing system, but it would not be a country for a gentleman, and I for one would be quite a stranger in it' (Pelling, 1955).

Temporary and operational, the American world was epitomised in an exclamation of one of Nathaniel Hawthorne's characters: 'What slaves we are to by-gone times —to Death, if we give the matter the right word.' Hawthorne suggested that public buildings should be built to last only twenty years 'as a hint to people to examine and reform the institutions which they symbolise'. The mood was also caught by the English educational investigator, Bishop Fraser:

'Progress under the direction of an educated *minority*', it has recently been said, is just now the maximum of desire on the part of most moderate-minded Englishmen, progress under the direction of the majority, whether educated or not, is the necessity of Americans.

(Fraser, 1867, pp. 169–70)

Fraser, as we have seen, reported on American schools for the Endowed Schools Commission in 1865.

American practice was also cited before the Cross

Commission (1886–8), by E. F. McCarthy, whilst the Bryce Commission on Secondary Education (1894–5), utilised the services of J. J. Findlay, who was to become a leading English interpreter of the ideas of John Dewey (VI—VII, pp. 339–407).

At the same time, Michael Sadler was appointed head of the Department of Special Inquiries and Reports, an imitation of the United States National Bureau of Education, a unique American intelligence service established by Henry Barnard in 1867. Under Barnard and his three successors, John Eaton (1870–86), Nathaniel Dawson (1886–9) and William T. Harris (1889–1906), it built up such a tradition of inquiry and report that its English counterpart did the same, acknowledging paternity in several reports. None can read volumes IX, X or XI without realising how strong American influence had become by this time in English life (Higginson, 1955).

Such influence was best symbolised by the name of John Dewey. First edited for English consumption by J. J. Findlay, Dewey's persuasive championship of the school as a rehearsal area for adult life (and therefore needing similar elected rulers and advocates) made an increasing appeal. His concept of it as 'an embryonic community life, active with types of occupations that reflect the life of the larger society and permeated throughout with the spirit of art, history and science', was very attractive, since, by selecting only the best elements in this adult life for acting out, the best would be reinforced, and the school could become a reconciliation centre for class tensions and group loyalties.

Dewey was the prophet of the rehabilitation of cities whose size and population de Tocqueville had regarded as 'a real danger' to future security. *School and Society* (1899) was really about how to educate for the city by turning the school into an urban community where communication only was studied.

(v)

Concern for the care of the sub-normal led to the dispatch to America as early as 1834 of a mission to investigate orphanages, homes for juvenile offenders, asylums for the deaf and dumb, poorhouses and prisons (Abdy, 1835). And as American society became more complex, crimes diversified and even more sophisticated techniques for coping with and correcting them emerged. Similar visits, culminating in that of Sir Evelyn Ruggles-Brise, led to the adoption of more permissively therapeutic techniques for the treatment of offenders between the ages of sixteen and twenty-one. Out of this evolved the Borstals, named from the first experiment in Kent.

Other American practices, like the playground movement and milk for children, were cited as worthy of emulation by an Interdepartmental Committee on Physical Deterioration which reported in 1904. It noted the effectiveness of the playground as a prophylactic for the asphalt deserts of the American city, especially in Chicago where Hull House, starting in 1892, led eleven years later to ten such parks in the southern suburbs of that city being laid out on the proceeds of a 5 million dollar bond issue. These American playgrounds catered for indoor as well as outdoor recreations and were staffed by 'organisers' or 'leaders'. And these 'leaders' were seen to be the vital elements in the movement. For, as Seebohm Rowntree told the Interdepartmental Committee on Physical Deterioration, open spaces would be 'of very small value, unless there is someone in charge'. He went on:

> In America, for instance in Boston, there is no single open space which has not got one or two men and women who have had experience of kindergarten methods, and who organise the play for the children. That is growing enormously in American cities; they are spending considerable sums. They see the need for

really organising play just as a matter in a better class school.

(H.M.S.O. Cd 2210, 1904, QQ 5134, 5138)

As with playgrounds, so with milk for small children, the case was strengthened by American practice. The professor of pediatrics at Harvard—the first to hold such a title in America, Dr. T. M. Rotch—was responsible for setting up a milk laboratory in London, as Dr. Vincent, who brought his work to the notice of the Interdepartmental Committee on Physical Deterioration in 1904, acknowledged (p. 44).

But the most spectacular contribution was that of Homer Lane, who, having heard John Dewey lecture on 'Schoolwork and Everyday Experience', migrated to Detroit in 1904 at the age of twenty-nine to teach handwork to a young Jewish boys' club and put Dewey's ideas into practice by organising them on self-governing lines. Not only were a number of other clubs formed, but Lane was asked to act as superintendent of a probation hostel founded by an Englishwoman. Soon after, it moved twenty miles into the country outside Detroit where, under Lane's consistent use of 'self-determination' in the treatment of delinquency, it became the Ford Republic. A celebrated sociologist at nearby Ann Arbor, Charles H. Cooley, expressed himself as 'heartily in sympathy' with Lane's ideas. More practical sympathy came from the Fords (not the motor car family), in the shape of financial grants of 45,000 dollars to enable Lane to compile a minuscule republic modelled on that of the U.S.A. Its members were 'citizens' under elected officers, paid for work they did and paying for things they wanted, including their board and lodgings. They kept their own time-cards.

He was invited in 1913 to come to England by George Montagu, later the ninth Earl of Sandwich, a penologist, whose distaste for the unnatural conditions of prison life led him to study American techniques of permissive therapy as practised by 'Daddy' George and his Junior Republic at Freeville, New York, and Homer Lane's Ford Republic outside Detroit. Lane was soon asked to run Sandwich's reformatory as a Little Commonwealth. Helped by Miss Bazeley—a former lecturer at Whitelands Training College—the Little Commonwealth was four years later certified by the Home Office as a reformatory for forty-five children. Some of his devices, like aluminium currency for paying the members on Flowers Farm in Dorset where the Little Commonwealth took shape, were adopted and adapted in public schools like Rugby and Rencomb (Simpson, 1954).

Lane fused the ideas of Dewey and Freud, telling Miss Bazeley on 24 June 1918 that 'he had been trying to out-Freud Freud'. He cast a spell over other prominent Englishmen, among them A. A. David, headmaster of Rugby and later Bishop of Liverpool, H. H. Symonds, who edited his papers, and the Rev. Dick Sheppard. Indeed, Lord Lytton, the Viceroy of India, regarded him as 'the most profound psychologist of his age and the greatest asset that any country can possess' (Wills, 1964, p. 207).

In the 'progressive schools' movement, perhaps his most distinguished disciple was A. S. Neill of Summerhill, who on Lane's death in 1925 in Paris became the exegete of the new friendliness between pupil and teacher. At the same time, S. R. Slavson, at Malting House School in Cambridge, was also acquiring psychotherapeutic insights into the therapeutic value of groups, later to be so brilliantly applied in the service of the Jewish Board of Guardians in New York.

The wheel had come full circle.

(vi)

Supplementing the intuitive therapeutics of Homer Lane and others, came the more rigorous Child Study

Movement, stemming from the stern scientism of G. Stanley Hall's report on 'The Contents of Children's Minds upon entering School' in 1880.

Impressed by what he saw of its members at the Columbia Exposition in Chicago in 1893, James Sully returned to England to found the British Child Study Association. As its name implied, this encouraged teachers to study the individual child and seek advice on their more difficult pupils from inspectors, or from Sully himself. To meet their demands, the chief inspector of the L.C.C. secured a competent educational psychologist, Dr. Cyril Burt. Originally appointed in 1913 'for three years, but no more', Burt's appointment was made permanent during the first World War.

After the first World War, the broader fields of health, especially emotional and mental health, captured American attention. With the help of the Commonwealth Fund, experimental child guidance clinics were established in St. Louis, Dallas, Los Angeles, Minneapolis, St. Paul, Cleveland and Philadelphia. The last-named so impressed Mrs. St. Loe Strachey in 1925 that she asked whether the Fund would undertake a similar experiment in England.

The Fund responded by sending Mildred C. Scoville to England in June 1926 to investigate, following this up by inviting twelve key individuals to visit the United States, together with five English social workers. As a result, the Child Guidance Council was organised in 1927 in London, and a clinic, staffed by American trained mental health workers, opened in 1929. At the same time, courses in mental health were established at the London School of Economics. The Commonwealth Fund saw the project to maturity, then, after 1932 as it obtained native support began slowly to withdraw.

After the second World War the various English agencies responsible for this work—the Child Guidance Council, the National Council for Mental Hygiene, the Central Association for Mental Welfare and the Mental Health Emergency Committee—all merged into the

National Association for Mental Health: at last financially, if not intellectually, independent of the United States.

(vii)

A clearing-house for such ideas was provided in 1921, when the New Education Fellowship was formed at Calais. Its journal, *The New Era*, reflected its Atlantic flavour, for both European and American pioneers of the 'new education' were represented: Dr. Montessori (Italy); Décroly (Belgium); Claparède (Switzerland); Dr. Reddie (England); and Colonel Parker (U.S.A.). Indeed, the American experimental schools, with their powerful professorial exponents, helped the New Education Fellowship to get under way. Their contribution was such that during the war from 1939 to 1945 their members, with others from Britain and Australia, kept the Fellowship alive.

In 1926, Beatrice Ensor, the editor of *The New Era*, spent six weeks in America and returned to enthuse over their 'decidedly scientific approach to educational problems'. 'American educationists', she continued, 'are not satisfied to say that a child is dull or stupid; they find out why a child is abnormal' (VII, 1927, p. 100). Thanks to her visit, The Progressive Education Association of America appointed a committee of three to co-operate with the New Education Fellowship, whilst American techniques like the Project Method, the Dalton Plan, the Winnetka Technique, the Gary and Platoon Plans were publicised in the journal.

One of its most vocal supporters was Harold Rugg, who argued in his book, *The Great Technology: Social Chaos and the Public Mind* (1933), that if 'man applies the scientific method to Man–Man relationships as well as to the Man–Thing relationships and lives creatively as Artist as well as Technologist' a civilisation of 'abundance, tolerance and beauty can be ushered in'. Even *The New Era*, organ of the New Education Fellowship, commented:

His problem is the American problem, as it should be, and his solution is an American solution, as it might not have been. The Americanness of the discussion needs to be stressed for the appreciation of Professor Ruggs' splendid effort to find a way through social chaos.

(xiv (1933), p. 187)

Among the many experimenters in group therapy given publicity by *The New Era* was S. R. Slavson. By 1928, S. Ferenczi could say to a conference of psychoanalysts:

we have advanced enormously in public recognition and can boast of a whole host of adherents. . . . In America this host seems more numerous than in Europe; at any rate, I find a more widespread interest in psychoanalysis amongst people who have not had experience of analysis.

(1928, pp. 283–4)

Dewey's ideas of child-centred activity methods oriented to a social purpose, were brought into the mainstream of English educational discussion, if not of practice, by the Board of Education's Consultative Committee. It found the project method, as outlined to the committee by Dr. Raup 'and several of our English witnesses', together with the Winnetka techniques, 'very applicable' in primary schools. Its judgements on the applicability of these techniques to secondary schools were even more favourable, if one looks over the generation stretching from 1926 (the *Hadow Report*), to 1938 (the *Spens Report*), 1943 (the *Norwood Report*) and to 1959 (the *Crowther Report*). For the *Hadow Report* 'endorsed Dewey in practice but not in principle', and the *Spens Report* stressed (p. 149) that 'the special needs and intrinsic values' of a child's life should be satisfied by education at the secondary stage. Activity and experience were likewise endorsed but when it came to practice jettisoned the project method 'which even the authority of Dewey does not make . . . wholly acceptable' (p. 159). The *Norwood Report* considered that examinations should cease to be externally imposed, and should be replaced by an internally framed 'set syllabus and papers' by the teachers themselves. It agreed that the time had come for 'the real meaning of secondary education, the significance of child centred education, the value of the Grammar School tradition, and the difficulties of the present Secondary Schools' to be recognised and admitted.

(viii)

Most of these difficulties centred round 'selection' and 'rejection'. After examining American schools in 1925, a young H.M.I. concluded that 'their non-selective system was good'. His report later became the basis of the L.C.C. School Plan for Comprehensive Schools in 1947, for the inspector, Sir Graham Savage, had meanwhile become the chief Education Officer for the London County Council. Sir Graham had his misgivings about the deceleration of school progress in the two-tier system (six to fourteen, and fourteen to eighteen), and proposed, after consultation with teachers' organisations, that they should establish 'comprehensive' schools. This, he said, 'for two reasons: one, because they cater for every activity; two, because all children from a given area, regardless of ability, will go to them' (B. of E. Pamphlet No. 56, 1928). (*The Times*, 2 April 1965.)

The absorptive process continues up to the present day, for the early American attempts to replace class teaching by individual learning have done much to stimulate new ideas about the organisation of schools and mitigate the polarising effect of streaming. Thus Michael Young's and Michael Armstrong's scheme for a flexible school, issued in Autumn 1965 by *Where*, itself an indirect product of American consumer research, reflects the influence of Carleton W. Washburne and Sidney P. Marland, whose history of the Winnetka experiment they recommend as background reading for their proposals.

(ix)

Attempting to discover and match laws of learning and laws of human nature led to attempts to evaluate teaching methods. E. L. Thorndike denied the existence of a so-called general intelligentsia—which provided support for those who wished to dislodge the classics from their dominance. Indeed, the whole doctrine of transfer of training upon which such dominance rested was increasingly questioned as a result of experiments instigated by Thorndike, who lamented that 'It is the vice or misfortune of thinkers about education to have chosen the method of philosophy or of popular thought instead of those of science' (Joncich, 1962, p. 6).

Armed with statistical techniques, Thorndike's pupils probed into local needs on behalf of school boards, and were increasingly hired by them to do so. In the *Journal of Educational Psychology*, of which he was a co-founder in 1910, techniques for such surveys were rehearsed as well as reported.

Increasing analysis of the efficiency of existing communications between teacher and student revealed the wide differences between the capabilities of individual teachers and students. Such differences tended to be masked as schools became ever larger units. These larger units involved mechanising the testing process, and so S. L. Pressey began, in 1915, to devise a machine which would give and score a test. This was not the first, as 600 such devices are recorded in the U.S. Patent Office records between 1809 and 1936 (Kay, 1964, p. 7).

In taking this test, students seemed to Pressey to learn more efficiently. His points were not taken up at the time, since teachers were in considerable supply. But as the available supply was soaked up by the expanding schools

77

and colleges of the 'fifties, interest was kindled in the more sophisticated work of the Harvard psychologist, B. F. Skinner, showing that such machines, employed what he called operant conditioning.

The popularity of quiz games facilitated the adoption of mechanising such question-and-answer methods of learning.

Just as tests were boosted by the need to find officers for the U.S. Army in the first World War, so teaching machines were devised by the U.S. Air Force in great numbers to train service personnel in the second. After the war, the Air Research and Development Command of the Air Force devised subject matter trainers, and Aircraft Companies devised complex controlled performance instruments.

Such technology of teaching made immediate impact on the Britain of the 'sixties, carried forward on the strong current of American innovative effort whose industrial manifestations we must now survey.

7
Industrial undertow

(i)

This scientism was fed by the steady advance of American
industrial skills in England. It began with the arrival of
the Chief Engineer of New York, Marc Isambard Brunel,
at Portsmouth during the Napoleonic wars, where he de-
signed machinery to mass-manufacture ships' blocks, and
thereby helped speed the imperative turn-round of ships
of the line, since each one required 1,400 blocks. Brunel's
advent marked the recognition of a new technique, the
principle of mass-manufacture of interchangeable parts.
Another contribution he is credited with is the 'art of
presenting three-dimensional objects in a two-dimensional
plane, which we now call mechanical drawing' (Rolt,
1953, p. 20).

Other Americans offered skills, only to be refused.
Robert Fulton communicated with Lord Stanhope, himself
a builder of calculating machines and patentee of the
steam vessel, but failed to open up a correspondence with
the inventive peer. So he 'undertook the task of inducing
"some of the leading capitalists of London" to take a trip
on the river Thames in his steam-boat'. Finding the English
unimpressed, he turned to France and then withdrew to
America, where his steamboat was a great success.

Adoption of the principle of interchangeable parts was

accelerated by the U.S. government's fear of the British in 1794, when it commissioned Eli Whitney to manufacture large numbers of rifles for defence. This he did by devising 'jigs' as guides for tools to eliminate shaky hands or imperfect vision, and automatic stops to disconnect the task from the tool when the job was done.

Six years after Whitney's death, Cyrus McCormick made a mechanical reaper, which was continuously improved and subsequently mass-manufactured in Chicago. Twenty-one years after Whitney's death, Samuel Colt visited Whitneyville to place an order for 1,000 revolvers, pistols and the machinery that made them. This machinery was to be the basis of a factory at Hartford and another in London. In the same year, Aaron Dennison predicted that 'within twenty years the manufacture of watches would be reduced to as much system and perfection and with the same expedition that firearms were then made in the Springfield armoury'. Earlier, Chauncey Jerome had begun to swamp the English market with cheap clocks; then from Dennison's factories, first at Roxbury, then from Waltham, Massachusetts, emerged the first factory-made watches in the world. By 1851, Isaac Merrit Singer was doing the same for sewing-machines.

The impact of these applications of 'the American system' really registered in the Great Exhibition of 1851. *The Times* described the McCormick reaper (9 June 1851) as 'worth the whole cost of the Exhibition', and the Colt revolver (2 September 1851), as likely to revolutionise military tactics as completely as the original discovery of gunpowder.

Of the other American major award winners, the most significant was Goodyear Indiarubber. Its infinite possibilities, especially in shielding tender English feet from the weather, were such that the English scientist, Dionysius Lardner, apostrophised rubber footwear as 'seven-league boots . . . fitting emblems of Jonathan who, when he walks a step, necessarily makes the strides of a giant'.

These giant's strides were perhaps better epitomised,

not so much by the *New York Herald's* claim, on 17 June 1851, that the Great Exhibition itself was an American idea, as by the legend at the head of the American exhibits:

> Both manual and mechanical labour are applied with direct reference to increasing the number or quantity of articles suited to the wants of a whole people, and adapted to promote the enjoyment of that moderate competency which prevails among them.

(ii)

Marketers of American inventions first appeared in England during the Napoleonic wars. One such was Joseph Chessborough Dyer, who with William Tudor founded the *North American Review*, the first four numbers of which they wrote themselves. Migrating to Manchester after 1816, he introduced the fly frame and the tube frame. His business was the manufacture of the machinery which he had patented.

Dyer helped to found the *Manchester Guardian* and took part in most of the radical movements of the times. Long before Richard Cobden took up the cause, he made a strenuous and stirring speech against the Corn Laws, on 5 July 1827, and took an active part in a movement to reform the representative system of the country, advocating the use of the ballot some thirty years before it was actually adopted. The Manchester Society for the Promotion of Natural History was but one of the local societies which owed much to him. So did the Bank of Manchester, founded in 1828. When it stopped payment on 31 December 1842, Dyer lost £96,000. Nor was this the only sum of money he lost, for six years later when a Machine Works at Gamaches, Somme, France, failed, another £120,000 disappeared. The house he used to live in is now the episcopal palace of the Bishops of Manchester.

Dyer was especially interested in education. He described the English 'system, if it may be so called', as 'utterly inadequate to the wants and just requirements of the country nor have we any hope that it can hereafterwards be made commensurate with the wants of society'. In his *Remarks on Education* (1850), he wrote: 'I look on the "Ragged Schools" as beneath contempt—why insult the poor by calling them ragged. I submit that in a proper and healthy state of society there ought not to be any Sunday Schools for *secular* teaching.' His theory of crime was that the poor were incited to it 'by witnessing superflux'.

In his tract on *Democracy* (1859), he showed that he was still American at heart:

far from apprehending mischief from the increasing democratic influences among us here, I look upon their spread, and fair chance of ultimate ascendancy in the councils of the country, as being fraught with the most salutary consequences to the public welfare of the *entire British Nation*!

There remains a touch of prophecy about his opinion:

England, at no distant day, will find herself compelled to act in concert with despotic rulers and thus aid in the general enthrallment of European nations—which God forbid she ever should!—or else she must be prepared to meet the combined hostility of such rulers. In such an event, as sure as fate in its approach the American States cannot afford to look on and see England fall beneath such gigantic forces as enslaved Europe may bring upon her; and therefore, the United arms of England and America will form the only *shield* to human freedom left in the wide world, and they must be so united for their mutual honour and safety.

To fulfil this high task will demand a great effort:

If a benign civilisation is ever to be advanced, we must endeavour, as its prelude, to strip society of all *shams*. But this can only be effected when *mental power* shall become adequate to the task of reducing to silence all supercilious pretensions, resting on ancient prejudices, and alone conceded to high sounding titles. Whenever we find extensively prevailing in society opinions and feelings that are *not* based on moral principles, nor yet derived from clear intellectual discrimination, they should be freely probed and laid bare, and this too, without much concern for the sensibilities that may be shocked by the process.

He laid bare the common background of the high civilisation enjoyed by both England and America:

careful observers must have seen that they have had their *roots* in the freedom of their people. They are the only two great nations whose institutions are based on the system of public freedom.

Americanwise, he added a cautionary rider:

we must be on our guard against the extreme subtlety, the known plasticity, and the assumption of superiority so continually and everywhere displayed by the complacent gentry, self-styled 'of the higher orders'.

He pointed out the connection between the Northern cause and the reformers in England in his *Letter to the Honorable William H. Seward* (1862):

the slave holders' rebellion has been hailed by the aristocratic classes as an event tending to secure and prolong their practical ascendancy, so as to place their *order* above control in the State . . . To this end, above all things, it was necessary to excite hatred and fear of 'Democratic Institutions' and especially those of the

United States, lest, by the example of their prosperity at home, and expanding moral influence in Europe, the people here might become discontented under the *unlimited aristocracy* now so comfortably established as the rule in Britain.

Dyer is but one of several nineteenth century American industrialists who represent the resurgence back into Europe of a new dynamic, a dynamic which was subtly to refashion Europe into an Atlantean rather than a Mediterranean mould.

(iii)

Meanwhile, the factory opened by Colt in London had impressed an Inspector of Machines in the British Ordnance Department, who confessed that 'it was impossible to go through that works without coming out a better engineer' (Burn, 1933, p. 296). Soon afterwards, the inspector went to America to see the parent company, and as a result the British government bought a complete series of Springfield machine tools, and imported several of the best and most experienced American workmen to work them. This was the origin of the Enfield rifle.

At a contest of threshing machines in Paris in 1855, the American Pitt machine threshed 740 litres of wheat in the same time as a British machine threshed 410, a French 250 and a Belgian 150. At another contest in Budapest two years later, the McCormick reaper won similar prizes. At yet another contest in Chile in 1859 between British and American locomotives, the former took 37 5-6ths minutes to pull a given train over a specified length to the American 26 1-10th minutes. In that very year, *Living Age* ridiculed John Bright for leading a movement to 'Americanise England'. For Bright described America as 'enjoying physical comforts and abundances such as are not known to the great body of people in this country, and which have never been known to any country in any age of the world'. Bright's view was shared by Charles Reade, the English novelist, who described America as 'at this moment ahead of all nations in mechanical invention'. If confirmation were needed from an American man of letters, it could be sought from Walt Whitman. To him one week's issue of the Patent Office list 'illustrates America and American character as much as anything I know' (Oliver, 1956, p. 268).

A visit in 1853 to the industrial areas of the United States with George Wallis, the headmaster of the Birmingham School of Design, impressed Joseph Whitworth (deviser of the famous standard screwthread known by his name) with their capacity to devise automatic machines that dispensed with skilled labour.

'We would do well to imitate if we meant to hold our present position in the great markets of the world', (P.P. xxxvi, 1854), he sagely observed and recommended scholarships, £118,815 to Owens College, Manchester, and a further £60,110 to Manchester Technical School (now the College of Science and Technology).

British engineers invited an American, Zerah Colburn, to edit their new journal, *The Engineer*. Colburn shuttled across the Atlantic like a honey bee, exchanging information about the latest technological devices, returning to England to found and edit, from 1866 onwards, a second journal, *Engineering*. This was to be, until *The Times Engineering Supplement* was founded in 1905, a clearinghouse of ideas.

Engineering yet further stressed the importance of American examples to English engineers, and in one of Colburn's last editorials dated 9 April 1869, he wrote:

In the engineering and the engineering practice of the United States we can find a much closer parallel than is afforded in France or in Germany, and if there exists there a method of professional education which has by long experience proved itself good, it is thither that we may look for an example rather than in the Continental Schools.

(iv)

The challenge to British hegemony in the field of prime movers presented by the economical steam engine of George Corliss with its improved valves was such that fifty were at work in England by 1867. Three were in Woolwich Arsenal and one in the hardware factory of John Platt at Birmingham.

Platt thought he could fairly be described as 'the largest mechanical engineer in the world'. Giving evidence to a Select Committee, appointed in 1867 to enquire into the provision of secondary and technical instruction in England as a result of the poor showing of British exhibits at the Paris Exhibition of 1867, he confessed that it was 'the custom among machine makers in England to purchase inventions from the Americans and adapt them for use in this country' (P.P. xv, 1867–8, Q5671).

Two characteristically American energy slaves, liberated by the Civil War, made great strides in the decades that followed. The first, petroleum, was noticed by T. Sterry Hunt in a paper to the British Association for the Advancement of Science in 1862: three years after, Edwin L. Drake developed the technique of boring for oil instead of collecting the seepage on the surface and so unlocked another door in nature's treasury. Entry to this treasury was further facilitated by the discovery by Colonel E. A. L. Roberts of New Jersey that an underground explosion would liberate yet more, and his device, patented in 1864, prompted the opening up of pipe-lines by Samuel Van Sickie in the following year. Long-distance pumps enabled them to lace America and rationalise this vast industry, a rationalisation that produced the aptly-named Standard Oil Company in 1870, a creation of John D. Rockefeller.

The second energy slave, the kilowatt hour, impinged

even more directly on England. For the discoveries of Charles F. Brush began to be manufactured in Britain from 1880 onwards. Three years later, American investors formed the Edison Swan Electric Co. Ltd., to operate in England. A third electric lighting company, the British Thomson-Houston was formed in 1896, which made not only lights but railway equipment as well.

To America, as a member of the Royal Commission on Technical Education, went a disciple of Emerson who had obtained the English rights to manufacture the Edison dynamo: Sir William Mather. Characteristically, Mather paid his own expenses. On his return, he was one of the promoters of the Technical Instruction Act of 1889, which empowered the newly-formed county councils to levy a penny rate on technical education (Mather, 1926).

(v)

The most influential anticipatory and optimistic revelation of America's technological future was Edward Bellamy's *Looking Backward 2000-1887* (1888): 'the latest and best of all the Bibles', according to Mark Twain. It not only reached more readers than did *Uncle Tom's Cabin*, but it also evoked over sixty further books in elaboration or refutation. Mark Twain congratulated the author for making 'the accepted heaven paltry by inventing a better one on earth' (Smith and Gibson, 1960, ii, 622). The press-button world of Bellamy and his imitators seemed to be endorsed by Twain's own attack on the Arthurian myth in which so many Englishmen were concerned: *A Connecticut Yankee in King Arthur's Court* (1889). Bellamy's hero looks forward to the Boston of the twenty-first century, Twain's is carried back, ostensibly to the Britain of the sixth century, but as percipient readers saw, really to the Britain of the late nineteenth century. For 'Sir Boss', as Twain's hero was called at King Arthur's Court, represented a deliberate challenge to the

English tradition by employing electricity to outwit it. Twain encouraged his illustrator to use real models, like the Prince of Wales and the Duke of Devonshire, for illustrating his text.

So offensive were these American paeans to industry that William Morris wrote a rebuttal, *News from Nowhere* (1891), with the apt sub-title: 'an Epoch of Rest'. This envisaged a London purged of all industry, the House of Commons as a market-cum-compost-heap, and all traces of the industrial revolution vanished as if they had never been. Morris's wife followed with *Looking Ahead: A Tale of Adventure* (1891), in which she showed how the plans adopted to bring about an industrial millennium had only brought about a 'shoddy feudalism'.

Substance was accreting to Bellamy's supposed fable. Electricity was being applied to haul the underground trains then being built for Glasgow and London, and they were known as 'Yerkes' Jerkers' from the name of their American builder, Charles Tyson Yerkes. (Incidentally, an earlier American engineer, who laid the railway between Shepherd's Bush and Ealing, became the eponymous hero of our railway system—G. F. Train.) The newspapers registered alarm, and the *Daily Mail* ran, in June 1901, a series of articles by F. A. McKenzie. These were subsequently republished as a book with the revealing title *American Invaders* (1902).

Between 1890 and 1900, American exports to England (excluding food, drink and tobacco) had doubled, and in that total, iron and steel exports had quadrupled.

American penetration of the British Empire was even more startling. In New Zealand, for instance, their exports jumped from £200,000 in 1896 to £1,000,000 in 1901, and special commissions were sent to investigate conditions. Other commissions were sent to South Africa, and one of them reported in 1903, 'America is undoubtedly our most formidable rival, present and future' (Heindel, 1940).

(vi)

The identification of the American worker with Bellamy's Julian West and Mark Twain's Hank reflected his own endorsement of capitalism. 'I believe he loves it', said the German socialist Werner Sombart. Inequalities of wealth, social status and power could be overcome through work. This was unlike England, where the term 'gentleman, signified 'a man of no occupation'. Indeed, an English engineer visiting the States concluded that America was on its way to becoming 'the foremost nation of the modern world', a place, said another visitor, where 'enough' was described as 'the loneliest and least employed word in the . . . vocabulary'. This was because the barometer of success was spending power. 'The American', concluded a native psychologist, 'would rather renounce a pleasure entirely than enjoy it in a modest way' (Smuts, 1953, pp. 2–7).

Arthur Shadwell, a British doctor whose professional interests led him into the social diagnosis of the ailments he once treated, remarked:

> The principle of getting the best out of every man on the one hand and of giving every man the fullest opportunity to make the best of himself on the other is more in consonance with the American than with the English spirit. There is more alacrity to apply it on the part of employers and less opposition on the part of the men or of the trade unions.
>
> (Shadwell, 1906, pp. 398–9)

For America was known as the Republic of the Joneses. This was its real appeal. During the Civil War, a prominent English journalist gave that name to a mythical neutral area between the warring North and South:

It may be that its President is a . . . modern St. Simon,

a Latter-day Père Enfantin; and that here are the aspirations that were dreamt of in the New Atlantis, and Sir Thomas More's 'Utopia' and M. Cabet's 'Icaria' and M. Fourier's 'Phalanstère' are realised. Some of these days, he concluded, this shadow may surprise us all, by proving to belong to a substance of some magnitude.

(Sala, 1865, ii. 396).

A generation later, an equally widely-read English reporter gave it as his opinion that

Until our working people who have a vote determine to use it to compel Parliament to give every English workman's child as good an education and as fair a chance of making his way to a university career (if he is bright enough), as he would have if he emigrated to the United States, nothing will be done.

(Stead, 1901, p. 348)

(vii)

America also mechanised the entertainment industry. In 1889, after ten years of experiment, Thomas Alva Edison succeeded, with the help of the talented W. K. L. Dickson, in producing the first phonograph and the first real motion picture film. Four years later, he established the world's first film studio near his West Orange Laboratories. Peep-show parlours began to spring up all over the United States. Edison's success stimulated Robert W. Paul in England, Louis and Auguste Lumière in France and Max and Emil Skladanowski in Germany to create a European film industry that was able to hold its own against competition from America up to 1914.

Then high explosives became more important to England and Germany than celluloid. As American film companies found their Westerns, comedies and romances in great demand as distractions, so, to cope with the increasing demand, they migrated to the cheap sunlight of California. There, in Hollywood, Marcus Lowe purchased his Metro Studio, Carl Laemmle founded Universal City and the famous Paramount Studios began to straddle the centre of the town.

These film companies bought talent from all over the world and re-exported it on celluloid for profit, often in houses with American-type names—Astorias, Warners, Paramounts. So dominant a hold did they acquire in Britain alone, that the government introduced a law in 1927 obliging British studios then distributing American films to make a certain quota of films for themselves.

When the Bell Telephone Laboratories, amongst others, and another industrial scientist, Lee de Forest, devised techniques of making talking films, American film makers achieved an even greater monopoly, since the electrical companies bought up or made agreements with all the other existing technical systems in the world. Only the fence of the 'Quota Act' of 1927 and the patronage of the Empire Marketing Board enabled a British documentary group to earn such international repute under John Grierson that Robert Flaherty moved from Hollywood to join it. Moved in 1933 to the General Post Office, this group produced *Night Mail* (1936) with a poetic commentary by W. H. Auden. But three years later Auden was in America and after the second World War Grierson went too.

Redeployed for capturing domestic rather than cinema screens after the second World War, the American entertainment industry received enormous financial aid from American industry in general through the sponsorship system on television. With such aid it manufactured, showed and exported soap operas, westerns and documentaries that had, if anything, an even broader impact than the ever-widening screens of the cinema (Knight, 1959).

(viii)

For by 1929, the national income of the U.S.A. was equal to the combined income of the United Kingdom, France, Germany and twenty other countries. (Thomas, 1954, p. 227). Britain had over half its investments in the Empire, and relatively few in new laboratory-based industries of the American kind, like electricity and chemical engineering. So to supply the deficiency, American industries moved into Britain. General Motors purchased Vauxhall in 1927 and Fords built their own factory at Dagenham in 1929. Others followed: Monsanto Chemicals (now the largest Anglo-American concern of its kind), the purchase of Boots Pure Drugs (resold back to this country in 1933), Electrical and Musical Industries (1932), Proctor and Gamble (1930), Hoover (1931), Standard Brands Foods (1932), and Remington Rand Office Equipment (1937), until by 1940, 233 American companies were operating branch units in Britain. American investments in the U.K. totalled $530 million and manufacturing investments $275 million (Dunning, 1958, pp. 42-3).

After 1945, even more manufacturing units were welcomed to increase exports, relieve the strain on dollar imports, and satisfy the ever-increasing demand for American goods. New American capital has flowed into fields like petroleum refining, pharmaceuticals and industrial instruments. Here, their own research and development had already built up formidable expertise. Nearly $200 million was invested by American petroleum companies in their refineries at Fawley and Coryton.

Of the 100 most important U.S.-owned manufacturing firms in Britain, the parent companies devote more of their resources to research and development than the whole of British industry combined. This heavy reliance on U.S. research and development was seen by an English observer to have three possibly pernicious effects. It might inhibit independent research by British companies; it might be withdrawn if the U.S. parent firm found more profitable fields for investment; and thirdly, it might well inhibit the native demand for pure scientists and technologists (Dunning, 1958, pp. 173, 310).

(ix)

In 1947, the U.S. undersecretary of state for economic affairs recommended that a three-year grant to war-ravaged Europe should be made, and that steps should be taken to encourage a European economic federation like that of the Belgium–Netherlands–Luxembourg Customs Union.

Such a United States of Europe was endorsed by political resolutions in both Houses of Congress on 22 March 1947. Six months later the Economic Co-operation Administration (E.C.A.) was established under Paul Hoffman, who offered to place the fruit of American experience at the disposal of European industry. Sir Stafford Cripps agreed, and on 16 July 1948 a joint Anglo-American Advisory Council was set up, composed of representatives of employers and trade unions both in Britain and the U.S.A. for this purpose. Significantly, the American chairman was Philip Reed of the General Electric Company, formerly deputy to Averill Harriman for the wartime Lend Lease Programme (*Hansard* 28–9 July 1948).

The Benton and Moody Amendments to the United States Economic Co-operation Act, 1948, and the Mutual Security Act, 1951–2, enabled 100 million dollars of the funds appropriated by Congress to be spent in certain countries, on schemes intended to encourage a healthy and expanding economy by promoting the productivity of industry. Of this money, nine million dollars came to Britain for spreading knowledge of the best and most modern American techniques and practices throughout British industry. It also fostered the employment of technical advisers by research associations, as well as research into social and economic factors affecting efficiency (Cmnd 8776 and Cmnd 8918, 1953).

Though Anthony Eden did not think that British industry was 'in a position where we require advice from any country, however eminent, in the conduct of our industrial enterprise', and was supported by a former president of the F.B.I. who did not consider that Britain's industry needed any 'magic from abroad', events proved them wrong. For the industrial penetration of Britain by American techniques and products was currently being intensified by defence needs. The rocket had replaced the Colt as the innovative defence weapon because the planets (the plural is advisedly used) had supplanted the prairies as the Americans' goal.

(x)

Far from being able to compete, Britain not only had to repair the devastation suffered in the 1939–45 war, but was forced by the Berlin Blockade and the Korean War to make major contributions to European defence: some £4,700,000,000 during the years 1951–54. The adverse effect of expenditure of this size on the Government's Welfare programme led to the resignation of Aneurin Bevan and Harold Wilson. When a Conservative administrator took over from Labour in that year, 1951, its leader, Winston Churchill, told the House of Commons:

> I rely on the rapidly growing and already overwhelming power of the United States in the atomic bomb to provide the deterrents against an act of aggression during the period of forming a defensive front in Western Europe. I hope and I believe that this will deter; but, of course, I cannot make promises or prophecies, or give guarantees.

> *(Hansard, 5 March 1952)*

Such reliance increased as economies became more pressing and as America gained ground. For Soviet long-range missile weapons made the supporters of an independent British deterrent take even greater steps towards America, since to carry the hydrogen bomb, American rockets like Skybolt, then Polaris, had to be purchased in turn. This resulted in the dropping of the native British project, the T.S.R. 2.

The traditional feedback from armaments into civilian technology, so visible in the case of the Springfield rifle and the Colt revolver, is even more so in the case of electronics and rocketry. New metals, new heat-resistant ceramics, ever more microminiaturised circuits, new techniques of communication, new techniques of storing energy, indeed—an ever widening eddy of new technologies—all ripple from the American ballistic policy. And not the least of them has further extended their mass media—Telstar.

(xi)

Telstar's origin—the Early Bird Satellite System—presents exciting possibilities for Educational Television. At present 115 Stations in the U.S.A. are wrestling with inadequate budgets and taped programmes that are not nationally synchronised. So their most generous backers, the Ford Foundation, produced in August 1966 a scheme for a Broadcasters' Non-Profit Satellite Service. This envisaged four 22,300 mile high satellites, one hovering over each of their continental time zones and each servicing 12 channels. Three of these channels were to be used for primary and secondary schools, one for universities and one for general education. Six were to be reserved for commercial broadcasts and the last was to be a reserve or spare.

Though only a scheme, at present opposed by the Communications Satellite Corporation that has hitherto enjoyed a monopoly since 1962, its very drafting illustrates the ever more dramatic deployment of technological innovation in the service of popular education.

(xii)

The widening gap between European and American technology, especially in the fields of high-speed computers and space, led to the appointment on 27th November 1966 of the President's Scientific Adviser, Dr. Donald Hornig, as chairman of a special committee to survey the extent of the gap and the means of bridging it. This was composed of representatives of the State, Defence and Commerce departments, the National Aeronautics and Space Administration, the Atomic Energy Commission and the Council of Economic Advisors.

Some see this gap as a reason for the drain of technically-qualified Britons to the U.S.A. The extent of this drain, first plumbed by a working party of the Royal Society under Sir Gordon Sutherland in 1963, has increased so rapidly that on 23rd November 1966 the Ministry of Technology and the Department of Education and Science together set up a special fact-finding committee under Dr. F. E. Jones, the chairman of the Mullard Electronics group.

Americans in turn began to press for a consortium of Anglo-American industries involved in electronic and space research. Though this would pool information and greatly increase American investment in Britain, the scheme was coldly received in December 1966 by the scientific adviser to the British Government. (*Observer*, 11th December 1966)

8

Conclusion

To cope with the thousands that funnelled out into the west, new types of schools had to be built and new techniques of teaching in them improvised. So America became the first nation to face the problem of educating everybody. No American school, whatever its material drawbacks, could afford to confess itself a third-class waiting-room for adult life. It is no coincidence that many of the techniques that, with modifications, have been found so stimulating in our own new secondary schools were the Gary Plan and the Winnetka Technique (both worked out in districts near Chicago), the Project Method, and the Dalton Plan (Boyd, 1930). Of these, the Dalton Plan made by far the greatest impact upon English class-rooms, especially between the first and second World Wars. Among its great English champions were Dr. C. W. Kimmins, a stalwart of the British Association section (he was president in 1929), and for many years chief inspector of the London County Council (Kimmins, 1930); Aldous Huxley, who gave great publicity to the most distinguished English exponent of the plan, A. J. Lynch of West Green School, London; and Sir John Adams, whose *Developments in Modern Educational Practice* was widely read in the nineteen-twenties and thirties.

The peculiar strength of our island civilisation has been its power to apprehend and absorb the best of continental and transatlantic practice, and apply it empirically. Being empiric, we have not had such a formidable stock of exegesis and commentary upon our system as the Americans and Germans have had upon theirs. Perhaps this is due to the fact that we are aware of what we owe to them and do not like acknowledging it. Even today, one hears the argument advanced that social conditions in America and England are so different that American experience is valueless in England. But those who advance it forget that technological and cultural change are great standardisers; they forget that the complex interweaving of the civilisation of one country by another is effected, not only in the schools, but in laboratories, factories, shops, cinemas, boardrooms, learned societies, banks, churches, and even on the tennis-courts, racecourses and boxing-rings. America has helped the English to adjust their many-tiered, deeply-embedded educational system to the conditions of modern life. The American frontier, moving westwards, pulled at the class layers of English society. And as the frontier moved westwards, prairie corn destroyed the amateur English farmer and American inventions rapidly supplanted the expensive English handicraft worker. The very pace of American technological change precipitated the solution of social problems long shelved (or at best tentatively handled) in our own industrial areas.

Having no competitive institutions, like churches, to challenge the mystique of the school and the college, nor a tangible, visible, potent past to enfold and conservatise them, their schools and colleges could plan for an indefinitely expanding future, fostered and nourished by endowments that have had no parallel in the history of the civilised world. It was this stupendous munificence to universities which led Sir Michael Sadler to comment that 'education was one of the religions that Americans believed in'. As Sadler remarked in 1921, 'It has its orthodoxy, its pontiffs, it noble buildings. Education is the Established Church of the United States' (Sadler, 1921, pp. 454–5).

The God of such a church was visualised by Olaf Stapledon as 'the all pervading spirit of movement which seeks to actualise itself wherever it is latent. God has appointed the great American people to mechanise the Universe' (*Last and First Men*, 1963, p. 72). His imaginary cult of Gordelpus was based on energy or divine power, and its consolations dispensed by a sacred order of scientists.

(ii)

The 'mission settlements' of this 'sacred order' of scientists have multiplied since the second World War. Their parish magazines are the journals; their legatine appointments, the endowed chairs in American studies; their ecumenical councils, the international congresses; their Rome, the Centre for Advanced Study in the Behavioural Sciences at Stanford. That the latter should have been established in 1954 with a grant from the Ford Foundation is significant, for it is based on the mathematical and statistical techniques that are creating the brave new American world.

American social, as opposed to the natural, scientists have had a twofold impact on Europe. In the first place, they have brought into existence new fields of study that are anti-historical, and antipathetic to value and *a priori* judgements. Secondly, they are pro-hierarchical, stressing the inevitability of élites, bureaucracies and hierarchical power structures. They stress small-scale, incremental change, and reject ideologies that envisage major transformations of the political, social, or economic order; hence they are likely to reject radical solutions, arguing that the advanced Western countries are 'post-Marxian and post-socialist' (Rogow, 1965). Empirical, mechanistic, qualitative, analytic and operational, they apply

Münsterberg's assumption that applied social psychology is independent of ethical implications. Their motivational studies, questionnaires, and other yardsticks for measuring human attitudes and actions, have also become weapons for more commercial strategists of desire.

A regular alphabet of conforming techniques, stretching from Admass and Alcoholics Anonymous through bowling alleys, consumer testing, dieselised railways, electrical energy slaves, glass sky-scrapers, hi-fi, investment trusts, jazz, the Kinsey Report, launderettes, managerialism, national parks, oil fractionation industries, packaging, Queeg-type debunkings of naval virtues, Readers' Digests, synthetics, television teaching, weighing machines, the exodus of talent and youth cults to Zen Buddhism can be compiled. The comprehensiveness of this catalogue is less impressive than the speed and certainty with which an alternative one could be compiled.

Such 'applied conformism' has widened the gap between the American dream and the American reality. For the dream has become 'an instrument for blocking social action by the Government . . . in order that it can be handed over to the private decisions of private managements, trade associations and professional bodies who tell no one what they are up to'. Even that most indigenous of English events, the General Election of 1959, was fought by the Conservatives with a seven-year-old Democratic slogan and by Socialists with others culled from the works of C. Wright Mills and J. K. Galbraith. Little wonder, therefore, that a British journalist should urge that

> We who are being invaded should take a long clear look at American Society and try and separate the myth from the reality [since] The whole cloth of American society may suit the majority of Americans admirably —although that is not so certain as it once seemed. It could become a winding sheet, and not a very well fitting one at that, for a culture such as our own.

> (Williams, 1962)

(iii)

That 'winding sheet' should perhaps better be called an investment portfolio, for by 1962 American investment in Britain was ten times its pre-war total. Greater than that in any other country in the world except Canada, its rate of increase has jumped from 5·6 per cent to 13·6 per cent since the second World War and is likely to increase still more as the return on investments in England is a third more than on those in the U.S.A.

This means that patterns of working and consumption become increasingly American. One in twenty of British employees in the British manufacturing industries are working for Americans. Nine-tenths of the blades we use and many of the electric shavers are American. So are three-quarters of the feature films we see. Of our wives' foundation garments, two-thirds are American and of their cosmetics, half. Half the drugs supplied by the National Health Service are American, so are one-half of our cars. As Lord Francis Williams wrote in 1962,

> As of now, the social face that America presents for emulation by the world is not the product of education in any sense in which the word is commonly used in an intellectually adult society. It is the end result of the most sustained effort in applied conformism in the history of the world.
>
> (Williams, 1962, p. 78)

But, in fairness, it must be said that social criticism still wells up in schools and colleges, as the 'revolt' at the very university where Lord Francis Williams held a chair —Berkeley—indicates.

The American tendency to atomise and analyse, though accompanied by great rewards in the realm of movement and gesture in the form of automation, cannot be said to have paid dividends in the field of knowledge. Indeed, the very popularity of quiz programmes is said to be due to the satisfaction they afford of seeing the expert humiliated by the ordinary man. Geoffrey Gorer sees that whilst atomisation of knowledge might enable the specialist to be equipped with skills at an astonishing speed, it enhances apathy and passivity towards their society. He forecast that 'this apathy and passivity, if increased and accompanied by a further lowering of the calibre of those who make politics a career, might well leave them open to the manipulations of a self-appointed élite of social engineers' (Gorer, 1948, p. 113).

Gorer himself acknowledged the stimulus he derived from the American anthropologist, Margaret Mead, whose perceptive analyses of the growing-up process were in the best tradition of the school of American anthropologists that grew up after the first World War. Margaret Mead pointed out how, by contrasting cultures, the rôle of the school can be seen in greater clarity. As she saw it, there was no one 'image' of the American school, rather a 'conflict between the school oriented toward the past and the school oriented toward the future, with the seldom obtainable dream of a school which would hold the world steady'. She saw this conflict expressed in many forms, classics versus modern languages, academic versus vocational education, required courses versus selectives in which shared conformity to a common past is opposed to selectivity which is a preparation for an unshared future' (Mead, 1951, p. 13).

In the fifteen years since then, this conflict has intensified as America itself has been increasingly paced by Russia and has tended to look more kindly on selective, élitist systems of education in other countries. With this has come a more astringent approach to their own 'image'. Indeed, by 1966 an American research team found British teachers to be so much more 'child-conscious' and permissive and Americans so much more 'learning centred' than had been supposed that they concluded: 'perhaps each country is trying to emulate something that never was or is not any more' (*The Times*, 19 February 1966, p. 7).

(iv)

Today, the real American contribution to education has made itself apparent in the application of technology to the learning process. Since the Vienna Exhibition in 1873, when their 'maps, charts, textbooks and other equipment' (as at the Paris Exhibition in 1878, and the Melbourne Exhibition in 1880) showed, they have been breaking the cake of custom because they have had to educate the citizens of the most fundamentally technological civilisation the world has known. This technology, as the great American historian Charles Beard has seen, is 'a social dissolvent and readjuster', which 'must be brought into the mainstream of history', if that course of history is to be surveyed correctly and 'the dark imminence of the unknown future' is to be in any way penetrated (Beard, 1932, intro.).

To brace schools and colleges to take ever increasing numbers that press against their doors and walls, technological skills developed in industry have been so successfully invoked that though the Progressive Education Association closed its doors in 1955, America still provides a lead to forward looking elements in England.

Thus the Ford Foundation's work has led to the adoption of similar programmes by its English counterpart, the Nuffield Foundation, and in its attacks on the paring of curricula to meet new needs has also influenced the Schools Council, which, since 1964, is collating inquiries by teachers, dons and H.M.I.'s. Moreover the simulation techniques devised in industry for evaluation and analysis first spread to education in America, together with cost analysis techniques. One such experiment, conducted by the System Development Corporation, the Computer-Based Laboratory for Automated School Systems (CLASS) permits simultaneous instruction of twenty students. It also monitors their progress in record form for predictive purposes as well as coping with simple problems of registration and time-tabling (Gross & Murphy, 1964, 68).

'The growing pains of American experience, however much they may hurt, will provide lessons of great value' wrote two architects sent out to report on American schools (Ministry of Education Building Bulletin No. 18, July 1961, p. 102). They found a tiered system of secondary schools replacing the single comprehensive high school, something later to be officially recommended in circular 10/65 of 12 July 1966. They found such schools were no longer built as a series of classroom boxes strung along a corridor, but were responsive to new techniques, catering for classes of 100 to 150 students as well as providing individual 'work stations' or cubicles. They found a concern for viable size, best expressed by J. B. Conant's suggestion that the minimum output of an average senior high school should be 100 'graduates' a year. Apart from teaching machines and language laboratories, two other new technologies of the classroom have made an impact since then. The first is 'team teaching' based on a specialist with overall responsibilities, deploying part-time help and students in training, and coping with from 90 to 250 students, grouped according to the demands of th subject. As pioneered at Harvard in the 'fifties with Judson T. Shaplin, SUPRAD (School and University Program for Research and Development) was tried out in the Franklin School in Lexington, Massachusetts, and proved so impressive that by 1961 thirty per cent of the large American High Schools had adopted it.

The second, television, following the successful experiment conducted from 1956 to 1960 at Hagerstown, in Washington County, Maryland, by the Fund for the Advancement of Education, has inspired large towns like

Glasgow to do likewise. Under William Beaton, former secretary of the Scottish Film Association, cables were laid in the ducts built for the old tramway system linking 315 of the city's 400 schools to a central studio in Bath Street. At present it reaches 10,000 pupils studying mathematics and 25,000 studying French in primary schools and it is hoped to provide science for sixth-formers, social studies for the middle school and courses in hygiene for infants. As the result of a meeting in Glasgow of representatives of the city and six neighbouring education authorities, a working party will examine the educational, technical and financial implications involved in any extension of the Glasgow service to schools outside the city. London, Hull, Plymouth and Edinburgh are also considering introducing similar systems and one of the Lanarkshire schools nearest Glasgow, in Rutherglen, has been given a special micro-wave frequency so that it can pick up the Glasgow schools educational TV by aerial. Since it has helped Glasgow to overcome a shortage of over 1,200 teachers, it may well provide as important an experiment in Britain as Hagerstown was in the U.S.A.

Adoption of these two technologies will throw into sharper relief the need to scrutinise an emergent American profession—the full-time school guidance counsellor. The need for training them was recognised by the National Defence Education Act in 1958 which established sixty training institutes to produce them. Hence their numbers have more than doubled—from 11,000 in 1959 to 24,000 in 1964. Counsellors in America cope with those aiming for some kind of higher education with dropouts, early faders, and problem children. As Gordon W. Allport wrote: (Harvard Educational Review, 1962, p. 377)

The great social stabilizers of the past have vanished . . . No longer can one counsel within the framework of Victorian decorum, theological certainties, or the

Pax Britannica . . . The comfortable stabilities of culture, caste, the gold standard and military supremacy are no longer ours.

(v)

Like the homeostatic tortoise programmed to go forward and which does so by encountering and negotiating obstacles, America has developed in an operational way. What some of its historians regard as 'manifest destiny' is really the experimental, critical and co-operative, technique that generations have devised to tackle problems posed by an expanding frontier in an operational way. The two best known route masters, philosophers indeed, of this way of life were William James, to whom 'intellectualism' was 'vicious', and John Dewey, to whom all thinking comes out of something and is for something. Both saw ends as merely guide-posts in man's endless progress through time. Whether in the work process (as indicated by Frederick W. Taylor and Elton Mayo) or the life process (as sketched by Robert E. Park, or the Lynds) or the lag between them (as adumbrated by William F. Ogburn), this operational attitude has elicited ever more flexible techniques for opening up roads to tomorrow rather than looking back to lost yesterdays: it is anticipatory rather than Alexandrine.

These flexible techniques are currently being employed by those working with groups. And, aptly enough, the joint sponsorship by the Research centre in Group Dynamics at Ann Arbor and the Tavistock Institute in London of the journal *Human Relations* is a contemporary example of the process of which this book is an altogether too brief and cursory an account.

Bibliography

ABBOTT, J., *The Teacher, or Moral Influences Employed in the Education of the Young*, revised by the Rev. Charles Mayo, 1834.

ABDY, E. S., *Journal of a Residence and Tour in the United States of America from April 1833 to October 1834*, 1835.

ACTON, J. E. E. D., 'Lord Acton's American Diaries', *Fortnightly Review*, cx (1921); cxi (1922).

ADAMS, F., *The Elementary School Contest*, 1882.

ADAMS, F., *The Free School System of the United States*, 1875.

ADAMS, H., *The Education of Henry Adams*, Boston and New York: Houghton Mifflin, 1918; Popular Edition, Constable, 1928.

ADAMSON, J. W., *English Education 1789–1902*, Cambridge University Press, 1930.

AGAR, H., 'Anglo American Commerce in Ideas', *Saturday Review of Literature*, 7 May 1955.

ALLEN, C. K., *Forty Years of Rhodes Scholarships*, Oxford University Press, 1944.

ALLOTT, K. (ed.), *Five Uncollected Essays of Matthew Arnold*, Liverpool University Press, 1953.

ALLPORT, G. W., *Harvard Educational Review*, xxii (1962).

ARMYTAGE, W. H. G., 'James Stuart's journey up the Mississippi in 1830', *Mid America*, xxxi (1949).

ARMYTAGE, W. H. G., 'Richard Cobden in Illinois', *Journal of the Illinois Historical Society*, xliii (1950).

ARNOLD, M., *Culture and Anarchy*, (ed.), Cambridge University Press, 1932.

Arrangements for the Expenditure of Counterpart Funds derived from United States Economic Aid in Cmnd. 8776; *Programme of Expenditure of Counterpart Funds derived from United States Economic Aid*, Cmnd. 8918, H.M.S.O., 1953, which details the projects supported.

ASHBY, SIR ERIC, *Community of Universities: An Informal Portrait of the British Commonwealth*, Cambridge University Press, 1963.

ASPINALL, A., *Politics and the Press, 1780–1850*, Home & Van Thal, 1949.

AXON, W. E. A., *Annals of Manchester*, Manchester, 1886.

BAIR, M. & WOODWARD, R. G., *Team Teaching in Action*, Boston: Houghton Mifflin, 1964.

BARNARD, C. I., *The Rockefeller Foundation Directory of Fellowship Awards for the years 1917–1958*, New York, 1959.

BEARD, C. A., introd. to J. B. Bury, *The Idea of Progress*, New York: Dover Publications, 1955.

BEARD, J. F., *The Letters and Journals of James Fenimore Cooper*, Cambridge, Mass.: Belknap Press, 1960.

BEGGS, D., *Team Teaching, Bold New Venture*, Indiana: Unified College Press, 1964.

BELLOTT, H. H., *University College, London*, University of London Press, 1929.

BEVERIDGE, LORD, *Power and Influence*, Hodder and Stoughton, 1953.

BISHOP, I. L., *An Englishwoman in America*, 1856.

BLACK, E. C., *The Association: British Extra Parliamentary Political Organisation*, Cambridge, Mass.: Harvard University Press, 1963.

BLODGETT, H., *Walt Whitman in England*, Ithaca: Cornell University Press, 1934.

Board of Education Pamphlet No. 56, H.M.S.O., 1928.

BOYD, W., *Towards a New Education*, A. A. Knopf, 1930.

BOYD, W., *The New Era*, xiv (1933), 81 ff., 123 ff., 145 ff., 197 ff.

BRANFORD, C., *Phases of Opinion and Experience during a Long Life*, 1883.

BRICKMAN, W. W., *Foreign Students in the United States; A Selected Annotated Bibliography*, Princeton, N.J.: College Entrance Examination Board, 1963.

BRISTED, J., *America and Her Resources*, 1818.

BRISTED, J., *Hints on the National Bankruptcy of Britain, and on her resources to maintain the present contest with France*, 1809.

British Association for the Advancement of Science at Aberdeen, The, Report of the Fifty-Fifth Meeting, 1885–6.

BRYCE, J., *The American Commonwealth*, New York: Macmillan, 1897.

BRYCE, J., *University and Historical Addresses*, New York: Macmillan, 1913.

BUCKINGHAM, J. S., *America*, 1841.

BURLINGAME, R., *Machines that Built America*, New York: Harcourt, Brace, 1953.

BURN, D. L., 'The Genesis of American Engineering Competition', *Economic History*, ii (1933).

BURSTALL, S., *Impressions of American Education in 1908*, Longmans, 1909.

BURSTON, W. H., 'The Influence of John Dewey in English Official Reports', *International Review of Education*, vii (1961–2).

BUSHNELL, D. D., *The Role of the Computer in Future Instructional Systems*, Department of Audiovisual Instruction, National Education Association, Washington, D.C., 1963.

CAMPBELL, J. W., (ed.), *Analog Anthology*, Doubleday, 1964.

CAWLEY, E. H., *The American Diaries of Richard Cobden*, Princeton University Press, 1952.

COBDEN, R., *England, Ireland and America, by a Manchester Manufacturer*, 1835.

COLE, G. H. D., *The Life of William Cobbett*, Collins, 1924.

COLLETT, C. D., *History of the Taxes on Knowledge*, 1899.

COLLIER, P., *America and Americans from a French Point of View*, New York, 1897.

COLLIGAN, F. J., 'Twenty Years After: Two Decades of Government Sponsored', *Department of State Bulletin*, xxxix (1958).

Commonwealth Fund: Historical Sketch 1918–1962, The, New York: Commonwealth Fund, 1963.

COOK, E. T., and WEDDERBURN, A., *The Works of John Ruskin*, George Allen, 1908, xxxiv.

CRAIGIE, P. G., *Report on Agricultural Colleges and Experimental Stations of the U.S.A.*, E 7699, H.M.S.O., 1895.

CRANE, V. W., *Benjamin Franklin and a Rising People*, Boston: Little Brown, 1954.

CROSS, B. M., (ed.), *The Educated Woman in America*, New York: Teachers College, Columbia University, 1965.

CURTI, M., *American Philanthropy Abroad*, New Brunswick: Rutgers University Press, 1963.

CUSHING, H., *The Life of Sir William Osler*, Oxford University Press, 1925.

DANIEL, H., *Public Libraries for Everyone*, New York: Doubleday, 1961.

DARTON, F. J. H., *Children's Books in England*, Cambridge University Press, 1958.

DICKENS, C., *American Notes*, Boston, 1867.

DILKE, C. W., *Greater Britain: A Record of Travel in English-Speaking Countries During 1866 and 1867*, 1868.

DOAN, E. N., *The La Follettes and the Wisconsin Idea*, New York: Rinehart, 1947.

DOBBS, A. E., *Education and Social Movements 1700–1850*, Longmans, 1919.

DUGGAN, S., *Observations on Higher Education in Europe* (Bulletin No. 3 Institute of International Education, New York, 1920).

DULLES, F. R., *Americans Abroad: Two Centuries of European Travel*, Ann Arbor: University of Michigan Press, 1964.

DUNNING, J. H., *American Investment in British Manufacturing Industry*, Allen & Unwin, 1958.

EDDY, E. D., *Colleges for our Land and Time. The Land Grant Idea in American Education*, New York: Harper, 1957.

FERENCZI, S., 'Gulliver Phantasies' in *International Journal of Psycho-analysis*, ix (1928).

FITCH, J. G., *Notes on American Schools and Training Colleges*, 1890.

FLEXNER, A., *Universities: American, English and German*, New York: Oxford University Press, 1930.

FLEXNER, S., *The Evolution and Organization of the University Clinic*, Oxford: The Clarendon Press, 1939.

FLEXNER, S., & FLEXNER, J. T., *William Henry Welch and the Heroic Age of American Medicine*, New York: The Viking Press, 1941.

FORMAN, M. B., *The Letters of John Keats*, (4th ed.), 1952.

FORSTER, E. M., *Goldsworthy Lowes Dickinson*, Arnold, 1934.

FOSDICK, R. B., *The Story of the Rockefeller Foundation*, New York: Harper, 1952.

FRANKLIN, H. B., *Future Perfect, American Science Fiction of the Nineteenth Century*, New York: Oxford University Press, 1966.

FRASER, REV. J., *Report on the Common School System of the United States and the Provinces of Upper and Lower Canada*, 1866.

FREEMAN, F. N., *Mental Tests: Their History, Principles and Applications*, Boston: Houghton Mifflin, 1939.

GODLEY, J. R., *Letters From America*, 1844.

GOHDES, C., *American Literature in Nineteenth Century England*, Carbondale, Illinois: University of Southern Illinois Press, 1944.

GOODENOUGH, F. L., *Mental Testing: Its History, Principles and Applications*, Staples, 1950.

GORER, G., *The Americans: A Study in National Character*, Cresset Press, 1948.

GOULD, J. E., *The Chatauqua Movement*, New York: State University of New York, 1961.

GRATTAN, T. C., *Civilised America*, 1859.

GRAY, H. B., *Public Schools and the Empire*, Williams & Norgate, 1913.

GRAY, H. B., *Eclipse or Empire*, Nisbett, 1916.

GROSS, R., & MURPHY, J., *The Revolution in the Schools*, New York: Harcourt, Brace, 1964.

HAMILTON, M. A., *In America Today*, H. Hamilton, 1932. *Hansard*.

HAULTAIN, A., *A Selection from the Letters of Goldwin Smith*, Werner Laurie, 1913.

Philadelphia: University of Pennsylvania Press, 1940.

HEINDEL, R. H., *The American Impact on Great Britain*,

HENNINGSEN, C. F., *Analogies and Contrasts*, 1848.

HENRIQUES, U., *Religious Toleration in England 1787–1833*, Routledge & Kegan Paul, 1961.

HETHERINGTON, A. L., 'The late Dr. Andrew Carnegie', *Library Association Record*, xxi (1919), 284.

HIGGINSON, J. H., *Sadler's Studies of American Education*, Leeds: Institute of Education, 1955.

Higher Education, Cmd. 2154 *Report*, H.M.S.O., 1963.

HILLCOURT, W., with OLAVE, LADY BADEN-POWELL, *Baden-Powell. The Two Lives of a Hero*, Heinemann, 1964.

HINSDALE, B. A., *Horace Mann and the Common School Revival in the United States*, 1898.

HOBMAN, D. L., *Go Spin You Jade! Studies in the Emancipation of Woman*, Watts, 1957.

HONEYWELL, R. J., *Educational Work of Thomas Jefferson*, Cambridge, Mass.: Harvard University Press, 1931.

HUGHES, T., 'The Youngest Anglo-Saxon University', *Macmillan's Magazine*, July, 1870.

HURLBUT, J. L., *The Story of Chatauqua*, Putnam, 1921.

HUXLEY, A., *Proper Studies*, Chatto and Windus, 1949.

Inter Departmental Committee on Physical Deterioration, Cmd. 2210, H.M.S.O., 1904.

IRELAND, A., *Recollections of George Dawson and his lectures in Manchester in 1846–47*, 1882.

JACKS, L. P., *My American Friends*, Constable, 1933.

JENKINS, R., *Sir Charles Dilke*, Collins, 1958.

JOHNSON, WALTER, & COLLIGAN, FRANCIS J., *The Fulbright Program: A History*, Chicago University Press, 1966.

JOHNSTONE, J. F. W., *Notes on North America*, Boston, 1851.

JONCICH, G. M., (ed.), *Psychology and the Science of Education. Selected workings of Edward L. Thorndike*, New York: Teachers College, Columbia University, 1962.

JONES, H. M., *The Life of Moses Coit Tyler*, Ann Arbor, University of Michigan Press, 1933.

KAY, H., in Austwick K (ed.), *Teaching Machines and Programming*, Pergamon Press, 1964.

KERR, C., *The Uses of the University*, Cambridge, Mass.: Harvard University Press, 1964.

KIMMINS, C. W. (in collaboration with BELLE RENNIE), *Triumph of the Dalton Plan*, Nicholson & Watson, 1930.

KNIGHT, A., *The Liveliest Art, A Panoramic History of the Movies*, New York: Macmillan, 1957.

KROUT, J. A., *Annals of American Sport*, New Haven: Yale University Press, 1929.

LARDNER, D., *The Great Exhibition and London in 1851*, 1852.

LEAVIS, F. R., & THOMPSON, D., *Education and the University. A Sketch For an English School*, Chatto & Windus, 1943.

LENNEP, W. VAN, in *Dictionary of American Biography*, xxii, Charles Scribner's Sons, 1958.

LEWIS, O. F., *The Development of American Prisons and Prison Customs 1776–1845*, Prison Association of New York, 1922.

LEWIS, R. W. B., *The American Adam. Innocence, Tragedy and Tradition in the Nineteenth Century*, Chicago University Press, 1955.

LICHTHEIM, G., *Europe and America. The Future of the Atlantic Community*, Thames & Hudson, 1963.

LILIENTHAL, D. E., *T.V.A., Democracy on the March*, Penguin Books, 1944.

LILLIBRIDGE, G. D., *Beacon of Freedom. The impact of American Democracy upon Great Britain*, (Paper back ed.), New York: A. S. Barnes, 1961.

LYMAN, R. L., *English grammar in American schools before 1850*, Washington, private edition distributed by University of Chicago Libraries, 1922.

MCGREGOR, O. R., 'The Social Position of Women in England, 1850–1914. A Bibliography', *British Journal of Sociology*, vi (1955), No. 1.

MACKAY, A., *The Western World*, 1850.

MCKELVEY, B., *American Prisons: A Study in American Social History*, University of Chicago Press, 1936.

MAIRET, P., *Pioneer of Sociology: The Life and Letters of Patrick Geddes*, Humphries, 1957.

MARTINEAU, H., *Society in America*, New York, 1837.

MARX, L., *The Machine in the Garden: Technology and the Pastoral Idea in America*, New York: Oxford University Press, 1964.

MASON, A. T., 'Business Organized as Power. The New Imperium in Imperio', *American Political Science Review*, June 1950, see also March, 1952.

MATHER, L. E., (ed.), *Sir William Mather*, 1926.

MEAD, MARGARET, *The School in American Culture*, Cambridge, Mass.: Harvard University Press, 1951.

MEDLEY, J. G., *An Autumn Tour in the United States*

and Canada, 1873; for his biography see *Minutes of Proceedings of the Institute of Civil Engineers*, lxxx, 1885; and *The Illustrated London News*, lxxxv, 1884.

MESICK, J. L., *The English Traveller in America 1785–1835*, New York: Columbia University Press, 1922.

MEYER, H., 'On the Heuristic Value of Scientific Models', *Philosophy of Science*, xviii (1951).

Ministry of Education, *Schools in the U.S.A.: A Report*, Building Bulletin No. 18, H.M.S.O., July 1961.

MONCKTON MILNES, R., 'Social Relations of England and America', in *Quarterly Review*, cxlii (1876).

MONROE, W. S., *A History of the Pestalozzian Movement in the United States*, Syracuse, 1907.

MOSCOWITZ, S., *Explorers of the Infinite, Shapers of Science Fiction*, Cleveland and New York: World Publishing, 1963.

Moseley Industrial Commission to the U.S., Report of the Delegates, Manchester, 1903.

MOTT, F. L., *A History of American Magazines*, vol. ii: 1850–1865, Cambridge, Mass.: Belknap Press, 1957.

MOTT, F. L., *American Journalism. A History: 1690–1960*, New York: Macmillan, 1962.

MUIR, R., *America the Golden*, Williams & Norgate, 1927.

MUNSTERBERG, H., *The Americans*, New York: McClure, Phillips, 1904.

MURRAY, H. A., *Lands of the Slave and the Free*, 1855.

National Association of Education Officers, *Education in Relation to Industry: A Report on Technical Schools in Canada and the U.S.A.*, Leeds, 1912.

Nature, i, London, 1869.

NEVINS, A., *America through British Eyes*, New York: Oxford University Press, 1945, (second edition, 1948).

New Era, The, 1932.

New York Industrial Exhibition: Special Reports of Mr. George Wallis and Mr. Joseph Whitworth, Parliamentary Papers xxxvi (1854).

New York Times, The, 1 February 1931.

OLIVER, J. W., *History of American Technology*, New York: Ronald Press, 1956.

PEARSON, H., *Conan Doyle. His Life and Art*, 1943, (Guild Books No. 224), 1946.

PEARSON, K., *Life, Letters and Labour of Francis Galton*, Cambridge University Press, 1924, ii, 345.

PELLING, H., *America and the British Left. From Bright to Bevan*, A. & C. Black, 1956.

PHILLIPS, G. S., ('January Searle'), *The American Republic Foreshadowed in Scripture*, 1864.

PHILLIPS, H. B., 'Charles Beard, Walter Vrooman and the Founding of Ruskin Hall', *South Atlantic Quarterly*, l (1951).

POPPLE, J., 'Adult education in Barnsley', *Notes and Queries*, cciv (1959).

POUND, R., & HARMSWORTH, G., *Northcliffe*, Cassell, 1959.

PRESSEY, S. L., 'A simple Apparatus which gives Tests and Scores—and Teaches', *School and Society*, xxiii (1926)

PRESSEY, S. L., 'A Machine for Automatic Teaching of Drill Material', *School and Society*, xxv (1927).

PRESSEY, S. L., 'A Third and Fourth Contribution toward the coming "Industrial Revolution"', *School and Society*, xxvi (1932).

PRIESTLEY, J., *Collected Works*, (ed.) 1817–1832, xxii, 40–54, xxiv, 7–25, xxv, 1–80.

Problem of Agricultural Education in America and England with special reference to a Policy of Developing the work at University College, Reading, The, Reading, 1910.

PROCTOR, M. R., *The English University Novel*, University of California Publications—English Studies 15, E. Berkeley: University of California Press, 1957.

Publications of the Central Society of Education, ii, 1839.

PUTT, S. G., (ed.), *Cousins and Strangers: Comments on America by Commonwealth Fund Fellows from Britain 1946–1952*, Cambridge, Mass.: Harvard University Press, 1956.

RALEIGH, J. H., *Matthew Arnold and American Culture*, Berkeley and Los Angeles, 1961.

RIGG, J. H., *National Education in its Social Conditions and Aspects*, 1873.

ROBBINS, C., *The Eighteenth Century Commonwealth*, Cambridge, Mass.: Harvard University Press, 1959.

ROGOW, A., 'American Sciences Abroad', *Guardian*, 24 August 1965.

ROLT, L. T. C., *Isambard Kingdom Brunel*, Longmans, 1957.

ROTCH, T. M., 'American Methods', *British Medical Journal*, 6 September 1902, 653 ff.

Royal Commission on Elementary Education, H.M.S.O., 1888.

Royal Commission on Secondary Education, H.M.S.O., vi–vii (1895).

SADLER, M., 'Education for Life and Duty', *International Review of Missions*, October 1921.

SALA, G. A., *My Diary in America in the Midst of War*, 1865.

SANTAYANA, G., *Character and Opinion in the United States*, Constable, 1924.

Schools Inquiry Commission, 1876, Vol. vii, Appendix xii.

Scrutiny, Cambridge, Deighton Bell, i (1932–3); ii (1933–4); iii (1934–5).

SCUDDER, T., *The Lonely Wayfaring Man. Emerson and Some Englishmen*, Oxford University Press, 1936.

Select Committee on Scientific Instruction, Parliamentary Papers, xv, 1867–8.

SHADWELL, A., *Industrial Efficiency. A Comparative Study of Industrial Life in England, Germany and America*, Longmans, 1906.

SHAPLIN, J. T., & OLDS, H. F. (ed.), *Team Teaching*, New York: Harper & Row, 1964.

SHIPLEY, A. E., *The Voyage of a Vice-Chancellor*, Cambridge University Press, 1919.

SIMON, B., *Studies in the History of Education 1780–1870*, Lawrence & Wishart, 1960.

SIMPSON, J. H., *Schoolmaster's Harvest*, Faber, 1954.

SKINNER, B. F., in *Proceedings of the Royal Society of London*, B.clxii, 1965.

SMITH, H. N., & GIBSON, W. N., *Mark Twain—Howells Letters*, Cambridge, Mass: Belknap Press, 1960.

SMITH, L. P., *Unforgotten Years*, Constable, 1938.

SMUTS, R. W., *European Impressions of the American Worker*, New York: King's Crown Press, 1953.

SPARROW, W. J., *Knight of the White Eagle: A biography*

of Sir Benjamin Thompson, Count Rumford (1753–1814), Hutchinson, 1964.

SPILLER, R. E. (ed.), *James Fenimore Cooper, Representative Selections,* New York: American Book Co., 1936.

STANLEY, A. P., *Life and Correspondence of Dr. Arnold,* 1890.

STAPLEDON, O., *Last and First Men,* Penguin Books, 1963.

STEAD, W. T., *The Americanization of the world, or The trend of the twentieth century,* H. Marckley, 1901.

STEPHENSON, G. S., & SMITH, G., *Child Guidance Clinics: A Quarter Century of Development,* New York: The Commonwealth Fund, 1934.

Stoke-on-Trent Education Department, *American Journey, A Study of American High Schools,* 1963.

TEWKSBURY, D. G., *The Founding of Colleges and Universities before the Civil War,* New York: Teachers College, Columbia University, 1932.

THISTLETHWAITE, FRANK, *The Anglo-American Connection in the Early Nineteenth Century,* Philadelphia: University of Pennsylvania Press, 1959.

THOMAS, B., *Migration and Economic Growth,* Cambridge University Press, 1954.

THOMAS, D. B., *The Origins of Motion Pictures,* H.M.S.O., 1964.

THOMSON, C. A., and LAVES, W., *Cultural Relations and U.S. Foreign Policy,* Bloomington: Indiana University Press, 1962.

THOMSON, P., *The Victorian Heroine. A Changing Ideal 1837–1873,* Oxford University Press, 1956.

THURSFIELD, R. E., *Henry Barnard's American Journal of Education,* Baltimore: Johns Hopkins Press, 1945.

The Times, 2 April 1965, 19 February 1966.

Times Literary Supplement, 3 January 1918.

Tracts for the Times No. 73, Ad Scholas, 1836.

TROPP, A., *The School Teachers,* Heinemann, 1957.

TRUMP, J. L., *Images of the Future,* Washington: Commission on Experimental Study and Utilization of Staff in Secondary School, 1959.

TRUMP, J. L., & BAYNHAM, D., *Focus on Change: A Guide to Better Schools,* Chicago: Rand McNally, 1961.

TWAIN, MARK, *Sketches New and Old*, 1900.

TYLECOTE, M., *The Mechanics Institutes of Lancashire and Yorkshire before 1851*, Manchester University Press, 1957.

University Development. Interim Report on the Years 1947 to 1952, Cmnd. 8473, H.M.S.O., 1952.

University Development 1952–1957, Cmnd. 534, H.M.S.O., 1958.

University Development 1957–1962, Cmnd. 2267, H.M.S.O., 1964.

VAIL, H. H., *A History of the McGuffey Readers*, Cleveland: Burrows Brothers, 1911.

VINCENT, E. W., & HINTON, P., *The University of Birmingham: Its History and Significance*, Birmingham: Cornish Brothers, 1947.

WAGENKNECHT, E., *Nathaniel Hawthorne: Man and Writer*, New York: Oxford University Press, 1961.

WARREN, HUGH A., *Technical Education in the U.S.A.*, London: City & Guilds, 1962.

WELLS, H. G., *The Camford Visitation*, Methuen, 1937.

WHITWORTH, J., & WALLIS, G., *The Industry of the United States*, 1854.

WILLIAMS, F., *The American Invasion*, Blond, 1962.

WILLIAMS, P., 'The Man Who Drives Minds to the End of their Tether', *Sunday Times Magazine*, 3 October 1965.

WILLS, W. D., *Homer Lane, A biography*, Allen & Unwin, 1964.

YATES, J., *Thoughts on the Advancement of Academical Education in England*, 1827.

YOUNG, M., and ARMSTRONG, M., 'The Flexible School', *Where*, Autumn 1965.

ZINCKE, F. B., *Last Winter in the United States*, 1868.

ZINCKE, F. B., *Why must we educate the whole people? And what prevents our doing it?*, 1850.

ZINCKE, F. B., *Some Thoughts about Schools of the Future*, 1852.

ZINCKE, F. B., *Inaugural Address to the Society for the Development of the Science of Education*, 1875.